Pr

LINSPIRED

Jeremy looks like a natural-born leader to me, having great relational skills, exhibiting strong character, and acting boldly. He's a great story for the NBA.

> **Pat Williams**, senior vice president of the Orlando Magic and author of *Leadership Excellence*

The explosion of Linsanity has been nothing short of extraordinary and couldn't have happened to a better man. Jeremy's story is the heartwarming faith journey that many have been waiting for in the NBA. You will be inspired!

> **Rebecca St. James**, Grammy Award–winning singer, author, and actress

There is no question that Jeremy Lin is an incredible basketball player, but even more importantly, he is impacting lives everywhere through his faith, hard work, and humble beginnings. It's hard not to follow the Jeremy Lin story.

> **Michael Chang**, tennis star

LINSPIRED

UPDATED AND EXPANDED

Jeremy Lin's
Extraordinary Story
of Faith and Resilience

MIKE YORKEY

ZONDERVAN®

ZONDERVAN.com/
AUTHORTRACKER
follow your favorite authors

ZONDERVAN

Linspired
Copyright © 2012 by Mike Yorkey

This title is also available as a Zondervan ebook. Visit www.zondervan.com/ebooks.

Requests for information should be addressed to:

Zondervan, *Grand Rapids, Michigan* 49530

This updated and expanded edition: ISBN 978-0-310-33751-5 (softcover)

The original edition was cataloged by the Library of Congress as follows:

Yorkey, Mike.
    Linspired : the remarkable rise of Jeremy Lin / Mike Yorkey.
    p. cm.
    Includes bibliographical references.
    ISBN 978-0-310-32068-5
    1. Lin, Jeremy, 1988- 2. Basketball players—United States—Biography.
    3. Christian athletes—United States—Biography. I. Title.
    GV884.L586Y67   2012
    796.323092—dc23 [B]   2012009218

Portions of *Linspired* previously appeared in *Playing with Purpose: Inside the Lives and Faith of Top NBA Stars* by Mike Yorkey and are used by permission. *Linspired* is based on research and interviews with Jeremy Lin but has not been authorized by him.

Published in association with the literary agency of WordServe Literary Group, Ltd., 10152 S. Knoll Circle, Highlands Ranch, CO 80130.

Cover design: Curt Diepenhorst
Cover photography: Robert Seale / Getty Images®
Photo insert design: Sarah Johnson
Interior design: Beth Shagene

Printed in the United States of America

---

13 14 15 16 17 18 /DCI/ 21 20 19 18 17 16 15 14 13 12 11 10 9 8 7 6 5 4 3 2 1

CONTENTS

Introduction | 7

1 Chasing the American Dream | 15

2 Where's the Miracle-Gro? | 29

3 Raising the Curtain on the Jeremy Lin Show | 41

4 Undrafted and Unwanted | 57

5 The Lockout | 79

6 The Miracle near 34th Street | 93

7 Leadership Written All Over Him | 111

8 Back to the Future | 127

9 Lessons from an Asian-American Trailblazer | 139

10 Linsanity and Tebowmania | 161

11 A Prayer Request for Jeremy | 171

About the Author | 185

Notes | 187

INTRODUCTION

For one delicious moment of time—just a handful of games in the middle of a consolidated, lockout-shortened NBA season—Jeremy Lin, a twenty-three-year-old Asian-American point guard for the New York Knicks, moved from anonymity to worldwide stardom faster than an outlet pass off a clean rebound.

In early February 2012, Jeremy was the last man coming off the Knicks' bench during garbage time; by Valentine's Day, his dribble drive through five Los Angeles Lakers graced the cover of *Sports Illustrated*; basketball pundits on ESPN SportsCenter had run out of superlatives to describe him; his No. 17 Knicks' jersey was the NBA's top seller; and media observers were declaring that he was one of the most popular athletes on the planet.

And then barely a month later, in an unexpected twist of fate, everything went *poof* when a knee injury ended Jeremy's Linderella season. It was the modern-day equivalent of a game buzzer sounding at the stroke of midnight and turning Jeremy's magical ride back into a pumpkin.

But who can forget how Jeremy galvanized our attention in a fragmented media universe when he progressed from an unsung benchwarmer to the toast of Broadway as the Knicks' leading scorer, playmaker, and spiritual leader. There was a wordplay on his last name that captured this Zeitgeist in perfect fashion: Linsanity.

What he did during a seven-game winning streak set the 24/7 social networking world on fire and created a tidal wave of tweets, touts, and online chatter about Jeremy's spin move from third-stringer to instant phenom. The reason Jeremy went viral was simple: everyone loves an underdog story, and his improbable journey had all the ingredients of a Hollywood fairy tale.

Trailblazing Asian-American in the NBA.

Harvard grad.

Cut by two teams and riding the pine in New York City.

Even the fact that he had been sleeping on his brother's couch on the Lower East Side of Manhattan was part of the lore. People imagined the poor guy sacking out in Josh's living room because there was no room in the inn.

I (Mike Yorkey) watched all this develop with great interest since I had been following Jeremy Lin since his rookie season with the Golden State Warriors in 2010 – 11. I was captivated by how this son of Taiwanese immigrants overcame preconceived ideas of who can and can't play basketball at the highest echelons of the game. He also impressed me with his levelheaded maturity and his willingness to talk about what his faith in Christ meant to him.

I interviewed Jeremy at length on two occasions following his rookie year and shared those thoughts in a book called *Playing with Purpose: Inside the Lives and Faith of Top NBA Stars*, which was published in November 2011. Keep in mind that this book was released almost four months before the launch of Linsanity, but we still placed Jeremy's picture on the cover—along with two-time NBA scoring champion Kevin Durant and 3-point shooting ace Kyle Korver—because of his "upside," as they like to say in sports-speak. Quite frankly, though, we were taking a chance with Jeremy by putting him on a cover of a book. Nobody knew what the future portended. The jury was still out on whether he would stick in the NBA.

Everyone was aware that Jeremy hadn't made much of an impression during his rookie season with the Golden State Warriors. He played in nearly as many games (twenty) for the club's D-League team, the Reno Bighorns, as he did with the Warriors (twenty-nine). When he was part of the parent club, he sat a lot. Many nights, the acronym DNP (Did Not Play) appeared next to his name in the box score. When he did see action, he averaged 9.8 minutes and scored only 2.6 points per game for a sub-.500 team that failed to make the playoffs.

Nobody was saying that Jeremy was the next Jerry

West, but I was fine with that. The fact that Jeremy even made it onto an NBA roster was noteworthy for several reasons:

1. At six foot three, he wasn't tall for a game dominated by humongous athletes who could have played on Goliath's team back in the day.

2. He came from an Ivy League school, Harvard University, which last sent a player to the NBA in 1953 — the year before the league adopted the 24-second shot clock.

3. He was the first American-born player of Chinese/ Taiwanese descent to play in the NBA.

The uniqueness of his story — his racial background, his Ivy League pedigree, and his undrafted status — were compelling reasons to feature Jeremy in a book about Christian ballplayers in the NBA, but those were surface explanations. What interested me more about Jeremy, after having spoken with him, was his deep reservoir of faith, his commitment to seeing himself as a Christian first and a basketball player second. Here was a polite, humble, and hardworking young man who understood that God had a purpose for his life, whatever that might be. He was in the midst of a wild, implausible journey with a leather basketball in his hands — and who knew which direction the ball would bounce?

"What kind of plan do you think God has for you at this moment?" I asked Jeremy, fresh after his rookie season in the late spring of 2011.

"I'm not exactly sure how it is all going to turn out," he replied, "but I know for a fact that God has called me to be here now in the NBA. And this is the assignment that he has given me. I know I wouldn't be here if that weren't the case. Just looking back, though, it's been a huge miracle [that I'm in the NBA]. I can see God's fingerprints everywhere. I just know that this is where he wants me right now. This past year, though, I have gone through a lot of different struggles and learned things that he wanted me to learn, to draw me closer to him, humble me, and make me more dependent on him."

When he uttered those words, no one knew about the mind-boggling odyssey awaiting him. We'll get to that, but first you need to read about his remarkable backstory: where Jeremy came from, how he was raised, and how this unheralded and lightly regarded prospect beat Lincredible—ah, incredible—odds to play in the NBA.

Chapter 1

CHASING THE AMERICAN DREAM

There are plenty of entry points for Jeremy's story, but a good place to start is by painting a picture of China in the late 1940s, when civil war ripped apart the world's most populous country. Chinese Nationalist forces led by General Chiang Kai-shek fought the People's Liberation Army—led by Chinese Communist Party leader Mao Zedong—for control of China, which at that time was a feudal society where a small elite class lived well and hundreds of millions barely survived. In 1949, after three years of bloody conflict, the Communist forces won, and Chiang Kai-shek and approximately two million Nationalist Chinese fled for their lives to the island of Taiwan off the coast of mainland China.

Among those refugees were Jeremy's grandparents on his mother's side. Jeremy's mother, Shirley ("Shirley" is actually an anglicized version of her Chinese first name), was born to a mother who was one of Taiwan's first prominent female physicians. One time during the 1970s, a contingent of American doctors visited Taiwan to study the advances that Taiwanese physicians were making in health care. As Shirley's mother made contacts with those in the American medical community, the seed was planted to immigrate to the United States, where the family could pursue a better life. In 1978, just after Shirley graduated from high school in Taiwan, she and the family moved to the United States.

Shirley worked hard learning English and later enrolled at Old Dominion University, a college in Norfolk, Virginia. Her major was computer science, a discipline with a bright future. Many felt the computer revolution would explode in the 1980s. A newfangled invention called the PC, or personal computer, was beginning to find its way into American homes.

There weren't too many Asians (or second-generation Asian-Americans, for that matter) at Old Dominion, and those who spoke Mandarin could be counted on two hands. The dozen or so Chinese-speaking students formed a small Asian support group for fun and fellowship, and one of those who joined was a graduate student from Taiwan—a handsome young man named Gie-Ming Lin, who had come to the United States to work on his doctorate in computer engineering. His ancestors had lived in Taiwan since the nineteenth century, long before Communist oppression began on the mainland in the late 1940s and early 1950s.

Sharing the same cultural background and a common language brought Gie-Ming and Shirley together, and they began dating. It wasn't long before their love blossomed. When Gie-Ming told her that his plan was to finish his doctorate at Purdue University in West Lafayette, Indiana, they decided to move together to Purdue, where Shirley would continue her undergraduate classes in computer science while Gie-Ming worked on his PhD.

Don't get the idea that these two foreign-born students had plenty of time to linger over coffees at the student union, attend a concert at the Elliott Hall of Music, or go sledding down Slayter Hill after the first snowfall of winter. Gie-Ming's and Shirley's parents didn't have the financial resources to contribute to their education, so they both had to work to pay their own tuition and living expenses. Shirley took shifts waitressing and bartending, while Gie-Ming moonlighted in his chosen field of computer engineering.

While at Purdue, Shirley was introduced to a Christian fellowship group and heard the gospel presented for the first time. Curious about who Jesus was, she began exploring and learning about the Lord of the universe and how he came to this earth to die for her sins. She fell in love with Jesus and got saved. When she told Gie-Ming what she had done, he investigated the gospel and became a Christian as well. They soon connected with a Chinese-speaking church and began their walk with Christ.

Gie-Ming and Shirley married while they were still in

school. They liked living in the United States and became two of the many millions of immigrants chasing the American dream.

They certainly weren't afraid to work hard—or live frugally. Early on, Gie-Ming and Shirley would go fishing on the weekend at a nearby reservoir. Behind the dam was a lake teeming with bluegill, shad, crappie, and huge bass. Gie-Ming, who loved fishing and was quite good at it, would catch his limit and bring home his haul in a galvanized bucket. They would eat some of the fish that night and toss the rest into the freezer.

And that's how the young couple would feed themselves all week long—from the fish Gie-Ming caught on weekends.

One evening, Gie-Ming flipped on the television to relax and came across a basketball game. The Los Angeles Lakers were playing the Boston Celtics during one of their great 1980s NBA Finals battles, and the sight of Larry Bird and Magic Johnson doing wondrous things on the Boston Garden parquet floor mesmerized Gie-Ming. He was smitten by the athleticism of these larger-than-life figures who made the basketball court look small. Gie-Ming started watching NBA basketball every chance he had, which wasn't often since his studies and part-time work ate up much of his free time.

Wait a minute—wasn't there a new technology arriving in people's homes back then? Yes, it was called the VHS recorder, and this then-state-of-the-art device could record television broadcasts on cassettes that contained magnetic tape. Suddenly, the images and sound of TV shows and sporting events could be played back at a more convenient time—or replayed over and over for the viewer's enjoyment. The advent of the VHS tape in the 1980s revolutionized the way Gie-Ming—and millions of Americans—watched TV.

Gie-Ming started taping NBA games, and he loved watching Kareem Abdul-Jabbar's sky hook, Dr. J's (Julius Erving's) gravity-defying dunks, and Magic leading the fast break and handling the ball like it was on the end of a string. It wasn't long before Gie-Ming was a certifiable basketball junkie. He studied those tapes with the same fervor he displayed when he studied for his PhD. He couldn't tell friends *why* he loved basketball, but he just did.

Gie-Ming also started playing a bit of basketball himself. He taught himself how to dribble and how to shoot by practicing jump shot after jump shot at a nearby playground. He was too shy to join a basketball league, but he could be coaxed into playing the occasional pickup game. He loved breaking a sweat on the basketball court, and playing the game became his favorite form of exercise.

After Gie-Ming and Shirley completed their schooling at Purdue, they moved to Los Angeles, where Gie-Ming worked for a company that designed microchips. Shirley jumped on the mommy track and gave birth to their first child, a son they named Joshua. Two years later, on August

23, 1988, ten years to the day after Kobe Bryant entered the world in Philadelphia, Jeremy Shu-How Lin was born.

A Westward Move

A job offer transferred the Lin family to Florida for two years, but then Silicon Valley lured Jeremy's parents, Gie-Ming and Shirley, to Northern California in the early 1990s. Gie-Ming's expertise became computer chip design, while Shirley—who had given birth to her third son, Joseph—returned to work in her specialty: quality control, which meant making sure new computer programs were bug-free when they were released.

The Lins settled in Palo Alto, a community of sixty thousand residents that bordered Stanford University. Gie-Ming, who wanted to introduce his favorite game —basketball—to his three sons, signed up for a family membership at the local YMCA. When firstborn Joshua was five years old, Gie-Ming introduced him to the fundamentals of basketball by using the passing, dribbling, and shooting drills he had studied on his VHS tapes. Jeremy received the same instruction when he started kindergarten, and so would Joseph when he reached that age.

When Jeremy entered first grade, his parents signed him up for a youth basketball league. But at that young age, Jeremy wasn't very interested in the action around him. He was like those kids in T-ball who lie down on the outfield grass and watch the clouds pass by instead of focusing on what the next batter is going to do. Most of the time, Jeremy stood at half-court and sucked his thumb while the ball went up and down the floor. Since he couldn't be bothered to try harder, his mom stopped coming to his games.

As Jeremy grew and matured, he eventually became more interested in basketball, especially after he grew big enough to be able to launch an effective shot toward the rim and watch it swish through the net. As shot after shot poured through the hoop, he was hooked. He asked his mother if she would come back and watch him play, but she wanted to know if he was actually going to try before she committed to returning to his games.

"You watch," he promised. "I'm going to play, and I'm going to score."

He scored all right. Sometimes Jeremy scored the maximum amount of points one player was allowed under Biddy Basketball rules.

For the rest of Jeremy's elementary school years, his parents regularly took him and his brothers to the gym to practice or play in pickup games. They also enrolled him in youth soccer, but basketball was the game he wanted to play.

As the demands of school grew, Jeremy and his brothers would do their homework after school and wait for their father to come home for dinner, and then everyone would head over to the Y at eight o'clock for ninety minutes of shooting and pickup games. Gie-Ming continued to stress the fundamentals because he wanted the game's basic moves to become second nature to Jeremy.

As Jeremy improved, he couldn't get enough hoops action. On many nights, he and his family practiced and played right up until the time they closed the doors at the Palo Alto Family YMCA at 9:45 p.m.

While basketball turned out to be a fun family sport for the Lins, they weren't going to sacrifice academics or church on the altar of basketball. Academics were important to Gie-Ming and Shirley because they had seen firsthand how education could give them a better life. Church was even more important because they knew what a relationship with Christ meant to them and to the spiritual well-being of their sons.

Wherever they lived, the Lins gravitated toward a Chinese Christian church. When they moved to Palo Alto, they found a church they immediately liked: the Chinese Church in Christ in nearby Mountain View. This place of worship was really two churches in one. There were services every Sunday morning—in Mandarin and in English —in separate fellowship halls. Several hundred attended the Mandarin-speaking services, while fewer people attended the worship services presented in English. The English-speaking ministry that the Lin family became involved in was known as Redeemer Bible Fellowship.

The strong demand for a church service in Mandarin was reflective of the demographics of the San Francisco Bay Area, home to the nation's highest concentration of

Asian-Americans. At one time, the United States census revealed that 27 percent of the people living in Pala Alto were Asian-Americans—racially identifying themselves as Chinese-American, Filipino-American, Korean-American, Japanese-American, or Vietnamese-American. There was a large Taiwanese-American community in nearby Cupertino (24 percent of the population), while other bedroom communities such as Millbrae, Foster City, Piedmont, and Albany had Asian populations of 10 percent or greater.

Stephen Chen, pastor of the Chinese Church in Christ's Redeemer Bible Fellowship, remembers the first time he met Jeremy a little more than ten years ago, when Chen was a twenty-three-year-old youth counselor. "Jeremy was around thirteen years old when I first ran into him," he said. "We were having a church cleaning day, and he was running around with his friends and being rambunctious. I remember scolding him, saying, 'Hey, we're trying to clean things up, and you're making things more messy.'"

Feeling chastised, Jeremy went home and told his parents he didn't want to go to that church anymore because the youth guy had been so mean to him. His parents didn't take his side, however, and the incident soon blew over.

Stephen Chen, who was always looking for things to do with the youth in the church, discovered that Jeremy and his older brother, Josh, were avid basketball players. Josh was starting to play high school basketball, and Jeremy was living and breathing the game in middle school.

"I hadn't played a lick of basketball before that time,"

Stephen said. "But I wanted to connect with the Lin brothers, so I asked them if we could do a little exchange: I would teach them about the Bible, and they would teach me how to play basketball."

Josh and Jeremy readily accepted. After the youth group meeting ended, they'd go to a nearby basketball court, where the Lin brothers taught Stephen how to do a layup, properly shoot the ball, and box out on rebounds. Then they would get the youth group together, choose up sides, and play basketball games.

"Jeremy would pass me the ball, even when the game was on the line," Stephen said. "He wasn't afraid that I'd lose the game for him. If we did lose, his older brother would get upset, but Jeremy would even console his brother. Even at that young age, Jeremy was hospitable, eager to get along with different types of people. He was also a natural leader, and kids listened to him."

Before entering high school, Jeremy wanted to get baptized as a public statement that he believed in Jesus Christ as his Savior and Lord. Stephen was pleased to hear of that desire. The Chinese Church in Christ had a baptismal font inside the church sanctuary, and Jeremy was dunked during a Sunday morning service. Not long after that, Stephen asked him if he would join the youth ministry's leadership team.

Jeremy was willing. The church had been renting a local high school gym on Sunday evenings so the kids in the youth group could play basketball and invite their friends to join them. "Jeremy would always be the one who would ask other kids to come out and play basketball with us," Stephen said. "And they would come. Jeremy wanted everyone to feel at home. That was just another way he extended kindness to others."

The gym had two full courts across the main court. Many dads saw how much fun their kids were having, so they would play too—fathers on one court, their sons on the other. Moms would visit with each other during the games of roundball.

All this basketball playing—after school, on weekends, and on Sunday nights—helped Jeremy to become quite a player, even though he was a shrimp on the court. As he entered his freshman year of high school, Jeremy topped out at five foot three and weighed 125 pounds. Jeremy had set his sights on playing high school basketball, but he knew that if he didn't grow a lot in the next couple of years, he wasn't going to get a chance to play, no matter how talented he was.

One day, Jeremy told Stephen, "I want to be at least six feet tall."

Stephen looked at Jeremy. He knew that Asians were stereotyped as a short people, and there was some truth to that. The average male height in the United States is five foot ten, while in China, the average male height is five foot seven. Unfortunately for Jeremy, his parents weren't tall either. Both stood five foot six, so he didn't have a great gene pool working for him.

"So how are you going to become six feet tall?" Stephen asked.

"I'm going to drink milk every day," young Jeremy replied.

For the next few years, Shirley was constantly running to the local supermarket to buy milk by the gallon. Jeremy drank the dairy product like it was … water. Jeremy had a glass of milk with his breakfast cereal, drank milk at lunch, and always had a couple more glasses of milk with dinner. He also gulped calcium supplements like they were Nerds candy.

"I drank so much milk because I was obsessed with my height," Jeremy said. "I would wake up in the morning and measure myself every day because I heard that you're always taller in the morning, at least when you're growing. I wanted to see if I had grown overnight."

Jeremy's great wish was to be taller than his older brother, Josh, who was in the midst of a growth spurt that would take him to five foot ten during high school. Desperate to will his body to grow taller, Jeremy even climbed on monkey bars at school and let himself hang upside down, thinking that doing so might expand his spinal column and make him taller.

Jeremy understood that he couldn't "force" his body to grow, but he also believed that to be competitive in the game of basketball, he had to grow to at least six feet.

And that was a tall order.

Chapter 2

WHERE'S THE MIRACLE-GRO?

When Jeremy moved up to Palo Alto High School, he made a big impression on his freshman basketball coach—even though he was one of the smallest players on the team. Years of playing in youth basketball leagues at the Y had honed his skills. His freshman coach stood up at the team's end-of-the-season banquet and declared, "Jeremy has a better skill set than anyone I've seen at his age."[1]

And then something miraculous happened.

Jeremy grew.

And grew.

And grew.

By Jeremy's junior year, he had sprouted *nine inches* to reach the magic number—six feet of height. He was still as skinny as a beanstalk, however, and weighed around a buck-fifty. The good news is that his growth spurt wasn't over. He would go on to add two more inches of height by his senior year of high school to reach six foot two.

Jeremy turned out to be a real late bloomer. He added *another* inch or inch-and-a-half during his college years to reach his present height, which is a tad over six foot three. He also added bulk by hitting the weight room. His body would fill out to a solid 200 pounds.

No longer the shortest player on the court, Jeremy showed his coaches and Palo Alto High opponents that he could run the offense, shoot lights-out, and make the player he was guarding work extra hard. His position was point guard, which may well be the most specialized role in basketball. The point guard is expected to lead the team's half-court offense, run the fast break, make the right pass at the right time, work the pick-and-roll, and penetrate the defense, which creates open teammates when he gets double-teamed.

When Jeremy dribbled the ball into the front court, he played like a quarterback who approached the line of scrimmage and scanned the defense to determine both its vulnerabilities and its capabilities. Jeremy's mind quickly calculated how an opponent's defense was set up and where the weak spots were. His quickness and mobility were huge assets.

His father, always ahead of the technological curve, had been filming Jeremy since his middle school days. He would break down the film, and then father and son would review what happened in his games. There was always something to glean from the tapes.

During his sophomore season, Jeremy was not only

good enough to win the point guard starting role, but his fantastic play also earned him the first of three first-team All–Santa Clara Valley Athletic League awards. His junior season was even better. Jeremy was the driving force behind the Palo Alto Vikings, helping the team set a school record for victories by posting a 32–2 record.

His coach, Peter Diepenbrock, recognized he had something special and turned him loose. He sat down with his player and said, "Let's tell it like it is. I'm the defensive coordinator; you're the offensive coordinator. Just get it done."[2]

Taking It Nice and Easy

Jeremy fearlessly pushed the ball up the court while playing for the Palo Alto High basketball team, playing an up-tempo game, but he was more cautious on the road when he was taking his driver's license test.

He flunked his first time out because he drove too slow – 15 mph in a 25 mph residential zone.

And that's just what Jeremy did in his senior year when he was the motor that propelled his team to the Division II California state championship. Going into the championship game, Palo Alto was a huge underdog against perennial powerhouse Mater Dei, a Catholic high school from Santa Ana in Southern California. No team had won more state basketball titles than Mater Dei, and the Monarchs, who had a 33–2 record, came into the game ranked among the nation's top high school teams.

Talk about a David-versus-Goliath matchup. Mater Dei was loaded with Division I recruits and had eight players six foot seven inches or taller, while Palo Alto had no one over six foot six. Playing at Arco Arena, home of the Sacramento Kings, Jeremy was all over the court, and he personally engineered the plucky and undersized Palo Alto team to a two-point lead with two minutes to play. Could the Vikings hang on?

Jeremy brought the offense up the floor, trying to eat up as much clock as possible. Suddenly, there were just seconds left on the 35-second shot clock. Jeremy was above the top of the key when he launched a rainbow toward the rim to beat the shot clock buzzer. The ball banked in, giving Palo Alto a 5-point lead.

Mater Dei wasn't finished yet, and neither was Jeremy. The Monarchs cut the lead to two points with 30 seconds to go, and then Jeremy dribbled the ball into the front court. Mater Dei didn't want to foul him because the Monarchs knew he was an excellent free throw shooter, so they waited for him to dish off to a teammate. Jeremy, however, sensed an opening and drove to the basket in a flash, taking on Mater Dei's star player, six-foot-eight Taylor King, in the paint. Jeremy went up and over King for a layup that gave him a total of 17 points in the game and iced the state championship in the 51–47 win. Palo Alto High finished their amazing season with a 32–1 record.

You would think that with all the college scouts in the stands for a state championship game, Jeremy would have had to go into the Federal Witness Protection Program to get a moment's respite. But the recruiting interest had been underwhelming all season long and stayed that way after the win over Mater Dei. It wasn't like Jeremy played for a tumbleweed-strewn high school in the middle of the Nevada desert. He was part of a respected program at Palo Alto High, and his coach, Peter Diepenbrock, was well-known to college coaches.

And Jeremy was highly regarded in Northern California high school basketball circles. He was named first-team All-State and Northern California's Division II Scholar Athlete of the Year. The *San Francisco Chronicle* newspaper named him Boys Player of the Year, as did the *San Jose Mercury News* and the *Palo Alto Daily News*.

Despite all the great ink and the bushel basket of postseason awards, despite sending out DVDs of highlights that a friend at church had prepared, and despite Coach Diepenbrock's lobbying efforts with college coaches, Jeremy did not receive *any* scholarship offers to play at a Division I school. That "missing in action" list included Stanford University, which was located literally across the street from Palo Alto High. (A wide boulevard named El Camino Real separates the two schools.)

It's perplexing why Stanford didn't offer Jeremy a

scholarship. After all, Jeremy checked off a lot of boxes for the Cardinal:

- great high school basketball résumé
- local product
- strong academic record good enough to pass Stanford's stringent academic standards
- Asian-American

Regarding the last bullet point, almost 20 percent of the undergraduate Stanford student body was Asian-American, and, as you read earlier, the school was located in a part of the country with a strong Asian population. But the Stanford basketball program took a pass. Some Stanford boosters interceded for Jeremy, telling the coaches that they simply *had* to give this Lin kid a look. But the best response the family received was that Jeremy could always try to make the team as a walk-on.

The Lins' eyes turned across the bay toward Berkeley, but the University of California coaching staff said the same thing: *You can try to walk on, but no guarantees.* During one recruiting visit, a Cal coach called Jeremy "Ron."

The disrespect continued at Jeremy's dream school —UCLA—where Josh was enrolled. Jeremy would have loved to have played for the storied Bruin program, and he was the kind of upstanding young man the legendary Bruin coach John Wooden would have loved to recruit back in the 1960s and 1970s. But the message from UCLA coaches was the same: *You'll have to make the team as a walk-on.*

Jeremy knew that few walk-ons—nonscholarship players invited to try out for the team—ever stick on a Division I basketball roster. He would never say it himself, but some basketball observers thought the fact that Jeremy was Asian-American cost him a Division I scholarship. Recruiters couldn't look past his ethnicity, couldn't imagine an Asian-looking kid having the game to compete against the very best players in the country. For whatever reason, they couldn't picture him playing basketball at the Pac-10 level.

Running Up Against a Wall

Jeremy had run into a "system" that blocked his path like two Shaqs in the paint. College coaches, who are the decision makers, look for something quantifiable in a high school player—like how tall he is or how high he can jump or how many points per game he scores. Jeremy's greatest strengths didn't show up in a box score. His game was running the show, leading the offense, and setting up teammates. He had an incredible feel for the game, a Magic-like peripheral vision, and a take-charge attitude that coaches love to see in their point guards.

"He knew exactly what needed to be done at every point in the basketball game," said his high school coach, Peter

Diepenbrock. "He was able to exert his will on basketball games in ways you would not expect. It was just hard to quantify his fearlessness."[3]

The problem likely stemmed from the fact that major college coaches had never recruited a standout Asian-American player before, so they didn't know what to do with Jeremy. Asian-American gym rats like him were a novelty in college basketball; only one out of every two hundred Division I basketball players came from Asian-American households. In many coaches' minds, college basketball stars had a different skin color or looked different than Jeremy.

The family had some options, however, thanks to Gie-Ming's and Shirley's insistence that their sons study and perform just as well in the classroom as they did on the basketball court. You could say that Shirley was a bit of a "tiger mom," insisting that Jeremy put as much effort into hitting the books as he did into improving his outside jump shot.

One time, Coach Diepenbrock received a phone call from Shirley, who had some distressing news: Jeremy's grade in a math class had slipped to a precarious A-. "Peter, Peter, Jeremy has an A- in this class. If it's not an A by next week, I am taking him off basketball," she threatened.

"Yes, I will stay on top of Jeremy," the coach promised.[4]

Thankfully, Jeremy righted the listing academic ship. Throughout high school, he carried a 4.2 grade point average (in the grade point system, an A is worth 4 points, but AP, or Advanced Placement, classes were weighted more heavily because of their difficulty) at Palo Alto High, where he had scored a perfect 800 on his SAT II Math IIC during his freshman year. Jeremy's parents felt that if Pac-10 and other Division I teams didn't want their son, then maybe he could play for a top-ranked academic college —like Harvard, for example.

The Lins looked east—toward the eight Ivy League schools, which are the most selective (and therefore elite) universities in the country. Harvard and Brown each stepped up. Both coaches said they would guarantee Jeremy a roster spot. Each made the case that they *really* wanted him to play for their basketball programs.

In the Lin family, there was no discussion. If Harvard —the assumed No. 1 school in the country in nearly everyone's eyes—wanted him, then he was going to play basketball for the Crimson, even if that meant his parents would have to pay for his schooling out of their own pockets. Harvard, like Yale, Princeton, Columbia, and the rest of the Ivy League schools, didn't offer athletic scholarships.

This was no small consideration for Jeremy's parents. In round numbers, a year of undergraduate studies at Harvard costs fifty thousand dollars, which covers tuition, room and board, books, fees, and the like. The Lins were already shelling out money for Josh's education at UCLA.

"The tuition is nuts," Jeremy told me in our interviews. "My parents did everything they could to get me through school. I received some financial aid from Harvard and took out some student loans."

"You were probably glad your parents stressed academics because you probably wouldn't have gotten into Harvard without being a strong student, right?" I said.

"Oh, definitely, I wouldn't have made if they hadn't been pushing me."

"Did they push you more in academics or athletics?"

"Academics. They were pushing for that."

Good thing that Gie-Ming and Shirley kept their eyes on the academics ball. Harvard turned out to be not only a great basketball school for Jeremy—where his game could grow—but a place that added to the Jeremy Lin legend.

By the Numbers

18: The number of Asian-American men's players in Division I college basketball (0.4 percent). This statistic comes from the 2009 NCAA Race and Ethnicity Report, which released during the time when Jeremy Lin was playing basketball at Harvard.

23: The number of students at Harvard with the last name of Lin while Jeremy was attending the university and playing basketball there.

Chapter 3

RAISING THE CURTAIN ON THE JEREMY LIN SHOW

Harvard basketball dates back to 1900, when John Kirkland Clark, a Harvard Law School student, introduced the game to the school just eight years after Dr. James Naismith invented the game at the YMCA Training School in Springfield, Massachusetts, eighty-eight miles west of Cambridge. On a wintry mid-January morning in 1892, the PE instructor nailed half-bushel baskets to the lower rail of the gymnasium balcony, which happened to be ten feet off the ground, and told his class that they were going to play a new game called Basket Ball. The objective: heave a lumpy leather ball into your goal. Good thing the lower balcony wasn't *twelve* feet, or we wouldn't have the NBA Slam Dunk Contest every year.

Harvard didn't have much to show for its 106 years of basketball tradition by the time Jeremy arrived on the Harvard campus in the fall of 2006. The Crimson had *never* won an Ivy League conference title, and the last time Harvard had played in the NCAA tournament was in 1946. In the four seasons prior to Jeremy's arrival, the Harvard team was 13–14, 5–22, 12–15, and 13–14. Winning seasons happened once a decade.

So it was no surprise that student apathy greeted the program. The mediocrity continued during Jeremy's first two years at Harvard (12–16 his freshman year; 8–22 his sophomore year), but both the Harvard basketball team and Jeremy were a work in progress. His coach, Tommy Amaker, who had been an All-American player at Duke and coached under legendary coach Mike Krzyzewski, liked Jeremy's quickness and his slashing moves to the rim, but the glaring hole in his game was his shooting beyond the 3-point line.

In college hoops, the 3-point line is 20 feet, 9 inches (it's between 22 feet and 23 feet, 9 inches in the NBA), so the guards are expected to keep defenses off balance by shooting the three—and making it nearly half the time. Jeremy, however, was a 28 percent shooter from beyond the 3-point line, and defenses noticed. They would back off to stop him from driving to the hole and dare him to shoot from beyond the arc.

At Coach Amaker's request, Jeremy focused on his outside shooting between his sophomore and junior years. Many mornings he met assistant coach Ken Blakeny at 7:00 a.m. to work on his stroke and increase his range.

The dogged approach worked. When he became a consistent threat to make the 3-point shot, the whole floor opened up to him. "That's why, in Jeremy's junior year, Coach Amaker basically gave him the keys to the bus and said, 'Let's go,'" said Will Wade, one of the assistant coaches.[5]

With Jeremy behind the wheel, Harvard basketball began emerging into the spotlight during his junior year, especially after Jeremy scored 25 points to help the Crimson beat a Boston College team that was coming off an upset of North Carolina. The team's improvement from 8–22 to 14–14 was significant, and Jeremy's numbers progressed just as dramatically: 17.7 points per game, 4.2 assists, and 40 percent from behind the 3-point line.

Even more noteworthy was the fact that Jeremy was the only NCAA Division I men's basketball player who ranked in the Top 10 in his conference in scoring, rebounding, assists, steals, blocked shots, field goal percentage, free throw percentage, and 3-point shooting percentage. He was improving quickly and becoming comfortable with his game, but Jeremy was also determined to live the life of a typical college student.

He lived in the dorms his freshman year and never put on the airs of being someone special because he played on the basketball team. Let's face it, at Harvard just about *every* student has a special talent in something, and Jeremy was no different. He liked making friends, hanging out, eating too much pizza, and playing Halo, his favorite video game. He was social, but he wasn't a partier.

Many young adult Christians lose interest in their faith when they go off to college, especially if they attend an elite, secular university like Harvard, which has been euphemistically described as a bastion of religious skepticism. Others get swallowed up by the nightly party scene and live prodigal lives.[6]

Jeremy, though, didn't step off the narrow trail that he set before himself. He knew he had to read the Word daily, so he made sure he was reading Scripture in the morning and in the evening before the lights went out.

"When I first got to Harvard, I was suddenly around athletes all the time, and I wasn't used to that," he said. "It's a tough environment, and if you don't have appropriate boundaries, you'll compromise your faith. I struggled spiritually for a while, and I didn't have many Christian friends. It wasn't until I connected with a small group during my sophomore year that things really started to change. I began to build a Christian community, learn more about Jesus in the Bible, and develop relationships that helped me with accountability."[7]

Jeremy also told me he had a cousin who was a pastor at a local church at Harvard Square, so Jeremy went to his church too. But joining the Harvard-Radcliffe Asian American Christian Fellowship (HRAACF), an Inter-Varsity chapter, really spurred his spiritual growth because he made friends he could talk to about his faith. He became a co-leader his junior and senior years, and although his involvement with the group was limited by the demands of schoolwork and playing basketball, he met regularly with Adrian Tam, an HRAACF campus staffer.

Adrian became a spiritual mentor to Jeremy as they studied the Bible together and read books such as Bill Hybels's *Too Busy Not to Pray.* "He loved his roommates, spending lots of intense one-on-one time with them, leading investigative Bible studies with them, and just plain hanging out with them," Adrian said.

What Tam remembers most about Jeremy, from their very first meeting, was his humility. "Even though he was more accomplished, smarter, and just plain bigger than I was, he always treated me with respect and honor," Tam says. "He was real with me, and he earnestly desired to follow God in all things. He had a quiet ambition, not only to be the best basketball player he could be, but also to be the best Christ follower he could be."

One of the best things about being involved with the Asian American Christian Fellowship was seeing fellow students come to Christ and make lifestyle changes, Jeremy said. "When that happens, you definitely see God behind it. I'm really thankful God is changing somebody, or sometimes he's changing *me.* To see that transformation brings me a lot of satisfaction and fulfillment. I definitely want to do something in ministry down the road, maybe as a pastor if that's where God leads me."[8]

Campus Life, Basketball Life

Following his freshman year in the dorms, Jeremy spent his last three years living at Leverett House, a student housing complex that overlooked the Charles River. He formed a tight-knit group of friends who lived together in an eight-man suite, with a common area for studying and socializing. When Leverett House formed a flag football team, Jeremy became the star wide receiver. During the 2009 Harvard intramural flag football championship against archrival Winthrop House, Jeremy proved himself to be quite a pass-catching machine in a 35–20 victory, leaping high for touchdown passes and interceptions.

If Jeremy showed no fear on the football field, he wasn't so brave when it came time for his annual flu shot. Alek Blankenau, a Leverett House resident and Harvard teammate, recalled the time when the basketball players were directed to get flu vaccinations at the start of the season — a sensible directive given how a flu bug can sweep through a campus. Jeremy was having none of it, though, because of a deep-seated fear of needles.

As the players queued up, Jeremy started to freak out. An agitated Jeremy whispered to Alek that he couldn't go through with it and wanted to step out of line. "I said, 'Are you serious? We're grown men. You need to get it together,'" Blankenau recalled. "That was definitely the most flustered I'd ever seen him."

He certainly wasn't as troubled on the basketball court,

where the first green sprouts of Linsanity pushed through the soil during Jeremy's final season at Harvard. His quiet ambition fully flowered on the basketball court, where Jeremy was a hit, pure and simple. The Harvard team rode his back to an unprecedented 21–8 record. As the Crimson kept winning games—and beating conference rivals like Yale, Brown, and Dartmouth—the 2,195-seat bandbox known as Lavietes Pavilion filled up with Harvard students wearing "Welcome to the Jeremy Lin Show" silk-screened across the front of their T-shirts.

Suddenly, showing up at college basketball's second-oldest arena (which opened in 1926) and cheering for Jeremy and their team was relevant again at an Ivy League college normally bereft of school spirit. Cheng Ho, the senior running back on the football team, saw a kindred soul in another Asian-American athlete on campus and sprang into action. He started a Facebook campaign called "People of the Crimson" to get people to come out to the Harvard basketball home games, which is ironic, since Facebook had started in Mark Zuckerberg's Harvard dorm room six years earlier.

Instead of the sparsely populated student section, Lavietes Pavilion was energized by a full house of spirited undergrads, curious alums, and even kids from the poor neighborhoods in nearby East Cambridge—with many of them wearing either "white out" or "black out" T-shirts (whole sections of fans wearing all-white or all-black) as directed by the latest Facebook post from Cheng Ho.

California Road Trip

During Jeremy's senior year, the basketball program at Santa Clara University, located fifteen miles from Jeremy's hometown of Palo Alto, invited the Harvard team to the West Coast for a "homecoming" game during Jeremy's senior year.

News of the matchup created a buzz in the San Francisco Bay Area.

"If you want to see an arena filled with thousands of Asian-Americans rooting for the best Asian-American basketball player ever, you should come to this historic game," wrote a blogger on the Golden State of Mind website, urging everyone to wear black in support of Jeremy's and Harvard's road uniforms.[9]

And come they did on January 4, 2010, when thousands of Jeremy Lin fans shoehorned into the 4,700-seat Leavey Center area dressed in their black T-shirts in support of the visiting team. The pressure of playing in front of parents and family, his old buddies from high school and youth basketball days, and his new fans took its toll. Jeremy suffered through a case of butterflies and scored only six points. He ran the offense well, though, in helping Harvard defeat Santa Clara, 74–66.

The reception was far chillier on the road, where college basketball crowds can be brutal. When the student section is not rhythmically chanting "bull@#$%, bull@#$%" after a call they don't like, they're dressing up in ways that mock the other team—such as wearing the clothes of Mormon missionaries (white short-sleeved shirts, black pants, thin black ties, and black bike helmets) whenever Brigham Young University plays on the road.

When the Sacramento Kings sharpshooting guard Jimmer Fredette was finishing up at BYU, the San Diego State fans gave him the full treatment. One fan held up a sign that asked, "Which wife gave you mono?" in reference to Fredette's bout with mononucleosis earlier in his senior season. But that was tame compared to the mean-spirited "You're still Mormon!" chants from the student section.

So it should come as no surprise that the sight of a prominent, all-over-the-floor Asian-American basketball player personally beating their team would prompt a few immature—and likely drunk—members of student sections to taunt Jeremy.

Some yelled really stupid (and racist) stuff, like "Hey, sweet and sour pork" or "wonton soup" from the stands. "Go back to China" and "The orchestra is on the other side of campus" were some of the other dim-witted taunts. One time at Georgetown, Jeremy heard terribly unkind remarks aimed in his direction, including the racial slurs "chink" and "slant eyes."

Jeremy showed God's grace and gave his tormenters the other cheek. But he also played harder. Granted, the catcalls bothered him at first, but he decided to let his game speak for itself. In the process, he helped make

Harvard relevant in college basketball and revived a dormant program.

Once again, he led the Ivy League in ten different offensive categories, as he did in his junior year. His scoring average during his senior year was 16.4 points per game, which is remarkable because he only took an average of 9.9 shots per game, a dramatic example of his unselfish play. For the third year in a row, he won Raymond P. Lavietes '36 Most Valuable Player Award, voted on by teammates. He set several records at Harvard: first all-time in games played (115), fifth in points (1,483), fifth in assists (406), and second in steals (225).

Jeremy's stock was never higher during his senior year than when Harvard played the then No. 12–ranked University of Connecticut, a traditional college basketball powerhouse, on the road. He dissected and bisected UConn for 30 points and 9 rebounds and threw a scare into one of the top teams in the country. Harvard lost 79–73, but Jeremy earned a set of new admirers.

The East Coast media heard of the Jeremy Lin Show and sent reporters from New York and Boston to check him out. They wanted to measure the player who had turned around such a dismal program.

Here are some of the more memorable quotes:

• "Jeremy Lin is probably one of the best players in the country you don't know about." (ESPN's Rece Davis)

- "He is a joy to watch. He's smooth, smart, unselfish, and sees the floor like no one else on it sees." (Boston Herald columnist Len Megliola)

- "Keep an eye on Harvard's Jeremy Lin. The fact that he's an Asian-American guard playing at Harvard has probably kept him off the NBA radar too long. But as scouts are hunting everywhere for point guards, more and more are coming back and acknowledging that Lin is a legit prospect." (ESPN NBA draft analyst Chad Ford)

Sports Illustrated did its first major feature on Jeremy in February 2010 in a piece titled "Harvard School of Basketball." Writer Pablo Torre zipped off this description:

It's a mid-January afternoon, and the senior econ major driving the unlikeliest revival in college basketball sits in his fourth-floor dorm room overlooking a frozen Charles River. He's surrounded by photos of family and friends back in Palo Alto, Calif., a poster of Warriors-era Chris Webber and an Xbox in disrepair. Nothing suggests Lin's status as the first finalist in more than a decade for the Wooden award and first for the Cousy award (nation's top point guard) to come from the scholarship-devoid Ivies.

"I never could have predicted any of this," says Lin. "To have people talk about you like that? I'm not really used to it."[10]

Torre was referring to Jeremy's standing as a finalist for the John Wooden Award, the nation's most coveted college basketball honor. Thirty players were nominated and ten were selected for the All-American team, but Jeremy didn't make the final cut after the end of the 2010 season. He had a better chance for winning the Bob Cousy Award as the nation's top point guard (named after Hall of Famer and former Boston Celtics guard Bob Cousy), but Greivis Vásquez, who grew up playing street basketball in the barrios of Caracas, Venezuela, received the honor.

When Jeremy's playing career at Harvard was over, and he had graduated on time with a degree in economics (he minored in sociology and carried a 3.1 grade point average), he had high hopes that an NBA team would draft him and give him a clean shot at making the roster. But there was a prevailing headwind he was fighting against —the fact that he didn't play in a major conference against the biggest, tallest, and best college players in the land.

His ethnicity?

Let's not go there, but the 800-pound gorilla in the draft room was that no Asian-American player with his background had ever worn an NBA uniform. If Jeremy was going to do it, he would have to be the first.

Many people don't realize how difficult it is reach the highest level of professional basketball. Approximately 3,600 men have played in the NBA since its inception in 1949, but how many have tried to get there—or imagined themselves wearing an NBA uniform? The answer has to be in the tens of millions, if you count every boy who pretended he was Michael Jordan or Magic Johnson or Larry Bird or Jerry West or Wilt Chamberlain in the driveway, dribbling the ball and driving toward the basket to score the winning basket in Game 7 of the NBA Finals.

Jeremy was one of those kids playing hoops for hours in the driveway. When he was in middle school, he and his brothers would stop playing and peer through the window when Dad had an NBA game on TV. Jeremy would see Michael Jordan make one of his patented fadeaway jumpers, and then he would return to their portable basketball standard to imitate the same move, over and over.

If you think about it, Jeremy was putting in his 10,000 hours of practice, the large round number that author Malcolm Gladwell (in his book *Outliers: The Story of Success*) claims is the key to success in any field—from playing a concert piano to becoming an ace computer programmer to becoming an elite athlete.

Jeremy had been practicing and playing basketball since he was five years old. By the time he graduated from Harvard, who knows how many hours he had toiled with a leather ball in his hand, working on all aspects of the game—shooting, passing, rebounding, and defense? It had to be way more than 10,000 hours.

Yet despite all the hard work he had put in to develop his God-given talent, the way Jeremy made it to the NBA came about in God's economy.

In other words, it was a miracle.

Chapter 4

UNDRAFTED AND UNWANTED

Ed Welland is a draftnik, the type of guy who sifts through statistics like a gold panner, looking for nuggets of key information.

Welland studied the crop of point guards on the 2010 NBA draft board and said the pickings for playmakers were going to be slim. "That doesn't mean there won't be a player or two who surprise the experts though," he wrote in the spring of 2010. "The best candidate to pull off such a surprise might be Harvard's Jeremy Lin. The reason is two numbers Lin posted — 2-point FG pct and RSB40. Lin was at .598 and 9.7. This is impressive on both counts. These numbers show NBA athleticism better than any other because a high score in both shows dominance at the college level on both ends of the court."[11]

This APBRmetrics stuff is way over my head, but what Welland was saying was that Jeremy's high field goal percentage inside the 3-point line — making six out of ten shots or .598 percent — along with his ability to rebound, steal, and block (that's the RSB40 statistic) made him a 24-karat gold prospect.

But what did Ed Welland know? He drove a FedEx delivery truck in the small eastern Oregon town of Bend and published his player assessments on the sports blog hoopsanalyst.com. When he chose Jeremy as his top point guard prospect, he had never seen him play because Harvard games aren't piped into lonely outposts like Bend. Welland made the call solely on the statistics printed on his spreadsheet.

NBA scouts put greater reliance on visual assessments, which are more subjective. In the run-up to the 2010 NBA draft, though, Jeremy got some long looks. He was invited to work out with eight teams, including his hometown Golden State Warriors. Yet when the big day came, Jeremy was passed over in the two-round draft, which selected only sixty players. Playing at an Ivy League school probably had a lot to do with that. The last Harvard player to wear an NBA jersey was Ed Smith, who played all of eleven games in his one-season career back in 1953 – 54. The conventional wisdom among pro scouts was that Harvard players just didn't pan out in the NBA. You had a better chance of becoming president of the United States; eight Harvard alumni have graduated to the White House versus four Harvard players making it onto an NBA roster.

Jeremy then caught a break when Dallas Mavericks' general manager Donnie Nelson invited him to play on their Summer League team after the draft noise settled down. NBA Summer League games are played at a frenetic pace, and they can be a bit sloppy, but for rookies and other nonroster players like Jeremy, Summer League provides a fleeting chance—perhaps a last chance—to pit their skills against NBA-level players and make an impression. This particular eight-day summertime season was held in Las Vegas in July 2010.

Jeremy wasn't a starter for the Mavericks' Summer League team, not by a long shot. He sat behind an electrifying point guard named Rodrigue Beaubois, whom Dallas coaches were evaluating for a roster spot. In the first four games, Jeremy was a spot substitute who averaged 17 minutes and 8 points a game.

Then some interesting things happened that changed the arc of Jeremy's basketball life. Look for the hand of God through this series of events:

1. Jeremy's team was playing the Washington Wizards Summer League team, which featured John Wall, the No. 1 overall draft pick in the 2010 NBA draft. Wall would be named the Summer League Most Valuable Player that season.

2. This was the last contest of the five-game Summer League season. A large number of scouts and NBA team officials were on hand.

3. Rodrigue Beaubois twisted an ankle and had a poor outing in the first half. Jeremy took his place.

4. By all accounts, Jeremy outplayed, outhustled, outdrove, and outshone John Wall in the second half while leading his team on a big comeback—drawing oohs and aahs from the crowd with several fearless drives to the rim.

Here's a thumbnail description of how Jeremy played: During the fourth quarter, Jeremy's tenacious defense on Wall forced a jump ball. He then came out of nowhere to make a sensational steal, then tore a rebound out of the hands of a seven-foot center. For the game, he hit 6 of 12 shots, including his only 3-point try of the night.

After that single half of brilliant play, several NBA teams looked at Jeremy in a new light. The Dallas Mavericks, the Los Angeles Lakers, and the Golden State Warriors all saw something in the kid. They thought that with the right seasoning, he could develop into an NBA player. Their thinking was that Jeremy could play a season in the NBA's Development League—known as D-League—and see where it might take him.

And then Joe Lacob entered the picture.

Who is Joe Lacob?

During the summer of 2010, Lacob was in the middle of purchasing the Golden State Warriors with Peter Guber, the former chairman of Sony Pictures. Together, they put out a $450 million tender to buy the team.

So how did this affect Jeremy?

Well, it turns out that Joe Lacob—living in the Bay

Area—had coached his son's youth basketball team, which had played against Jeremy when he was a pip-squeak. This fascinating exchange between Lacob and *San Jose Mercury News* columnist Tim Kawakami explains things:

Let's just confirm that you made the call to sign Jeremy Lin.

Lacob: It was my call.

Why Lin?

Lacob: Well, that's a special situation.

Your son played with Lin? Against Lin?

Lacob: There were probably three guys who were pretty much the best point guards in high school in this area at that time, and Jeremy Lin was probably the best of them. And my son, Kirk, was right there with him. I've watched them play against each other, and I've coached against him since he was this high.

So I know him from [the time he was] a little kid. Also at Palo Alto I watched him win the state championship over a superior team, and he dominated it. Mater Dei. And he has heart, he has a lot of talent, he's athletic, which a lot of people don't understand. He's pretty long.

He has a game that translates to the NBA. He can drive; he's a slasher. He needs to shoot better, obviously. He needs to be a better outside shooter.

It's funny, people don't know his game. They say, oh, he's a shooter but he doesn't have these other skills. No, that's not true, it's the opposite.

Jeremy Lin, I think, can play. He didn't sign because he's Asian-American. That was a nice feature, like anything else. And I think it's great for that community and for the Warriors. But he got signed because he can play.

If you watched his tape, if you watched him in the John Wall thing in Vegas, he played John Wall even up. This is not a guy who shouldn't have been drafted. This is a guy who should've been drafted.

Doesn't that put some pressure on a coach to play him?

Lacob: No, he's got to prove it on the court.

You'll be watching.

Lacob: That's not for me to determine. He has to prove it, coaches have to coach him, and we'll see. Jeremy should've obviously gotten recruited to Stanford. Made a huge error. And by the way, there were a lot of us who were Stanford boosters who were trying to get them to recruit Jeremy. They did not. Well, guess what, that was really stupid. I'm a big Stanford fan, but that was really stupid. The kid was right across the street. You can't recognize that, you've got a problem.[12]

And that's how Jeremy Lin got his chance to play in the NBA. Two weeks after Summer League, he signed a two-year contract with the Warriors, and the news of his signing sent a shock wave through the San Francisco Bay Area—especially the Asian-American community. Then, through tenacity and grit in training camp, Jeremy won a spot on the Warriors' roster.

Undrafted, fighting for recognition, and given the slimmest of opportunities, Jeremy had somehow beaten the incredible odds to put on an NBA jersey.

Even better, his hometown team wanted him—and so did the hometown fans.

His Rookie Year

After signing with the Warriors, Jeremy got his own place in Hayward, located roughly midway between his parents' home in Palo Alto and the Oracle Arena in Oakland, where the Warriors play.

Training camp, however, was a rude awakening. Jeremy discovered that he wasn't as ready for the big leagues as he thought. The level of play was faster, taller, and better. His teammates outperformed him in practice drills, which only heightened his anxiety and wilted his confidence. Even his coaches' encouragement couldn't lift his spirits. "I was humbled very quickly," he said, describing that rude awakening as a roller-coaster ride between euphoria and despair. He made the team, but just barely. Jeremy chose to wear No. 7—the biblical number that denotes completeness or perfection—as his jersey number.[13]

He sat on the bench for the season-opening win against the Houston Rockets but made his NBA debut two nights later in Golden State's second game of the 2010–11 season —on "Asian Heritage Night." A packed house of 17,408 fans exploded with cheers when he was inserted into the game with two and a half minutes to go—and the Warriors comfortably ahead. Jeremy had the honor of dribbling out the final seconds of a hometown win over the Los Angeles Clippers.

Jeremy Lin had made history, becoming the first Asian-American basketball player of Chinese/Taiwanese descent to step onto a ninety-four-by-fifty-foot NBA hardwood court. The only other full-blooded American-born Asian to play professional basketball in the United States was five foot seven Wataru "Kilo Wat" Misaka, who played in only *three* games for the New York Knickerbockers back in 1947—in the old Basketball Association of America (BAA), which would become the NBA two years later. Born to Japanese immigrants, Misaka deserves honorable mention for being a pioneer at a time when Americans had just defeated Japan in World War II and when memories of Japanese Army atrocities were still fresh in the public's memory.

More importantly, "Kilo Wat," who came along in the same year that Jackie Robinson broke the color barrier in Major League Baseball, was the first non-Caucasian to play professional basketball—a noteworthy achievement, since it would be another three years before the NBA admitted its first black player in 1950.

Over the years, there have been four other NBA players —Raymond Townsend, Corey Gaines, Rex Walters, and Robert Swift—who came from a mixed heritage, such as an American father married to a Japanese or Filipino mother. And then there are foreign-born Asians such as Yao Ming and Yi Jianlian.

I remember watching Jeremy play on TV during those early games with the Warriors. He hustled and played hard, but it was evident that he was playing not to make any mistakes, which makes a player less aggressive in a hard-nosed professional game where boldness and determination separate those who make it from those who are looking for a new job—like playing for an overseas team.

Jeremy's newfound notoriety added to the pressure. An immediate blast of attention came from the media heavyweights—*NBC Nightly News*, the *New York Times*, and *Time* magazine, to name a few—who wrote glowing features about the first Asian-American of Chinese/Taiwanese heritage to play in the NBA. Jeremy thought he was grounded enough to withstand this media examination, as well as the thousands of requests to "friend" him on his Facebook page, but he soon learned otherwise. Even though the local fans loved cheering for their native son, the focused attention created an intense spotlight that followed him everywhere, and it showed on the court. It was apparent that he was a work in progress as a basketball player.

In late December 2010, the Warriors reassigned Jeremy
—who had been averaging 8.5 minutes a game—to their
D-League affiliate, the Reno Bighorns. It was hard for
him not to see the move as a demotion.

In a state of near despair, Jeremy wrote in his personal
journal that he felt like a failure after putting so much
pressure on himself to make the NBA. During a conference hosted by River of Life Christian Church in Santa
Clara after the season was over, Jeremy said he wrote this
entry into his personal journal on December 29, 2010:

> *This is probably the closest to depression I've been. I
> lack confidence on the court. I'm not having fun playing
> basketball anymore. I hate being in the D-League, and I
> want to rejoin the Warriors. I feel embarrassed and like
> a failure.*[14]

If you think about it, Jeremy had never "failed" at anything before. He'd been a straight-A student, achieved top
scores in the SATs, attended Harvard, and turned himself
into one of the best college basketball players in the country. But the NBA was a tough nut to crack, which only
stands to reason, since many people say that the world's
best athletes play the game.

NBA players ...

- are taller and stronger than 99.999999 percent of
  the world's population

- can run like gazelles while maintaining a dribble

- can stop on a dime and successfully shoot a ball through a rim that has a diameter of 17 inches (about an inch less than twice the diameter of the basketball)

- show impressive athleticism and "hang time" when driving toward the rim

Basketball players must move quickly laterally, show great coordination, and jump like kangaroos. Put together, this creates quite an athletic package and underscores why the physical demands of professional basketball are higher than other major sports because of its robust combination of heart-pounding exercise and skillful shooting.

Jeremy had come so far—like pounding a high striker with a mallet and watching the puck rise within inches of hitting the bell. And now this, the nadir of his basketball career. "It was a shock [going to Reno] because I did not realize how different the two leagues were," he said. "It was also humbling because the locker rooms, facilities, attendance at games, the travel—it was all very different."

On New Year's Day 2011, he wrote in his journal, "I wish I had never signed with the Warriors."

Jeremy did some soul-searching and came to this conclusion, which he shared with the attendees of the conference at the River of Life Christian Church: "None of the paychecks, the car, the fame, none of the NBA lifestyle, none of that stuff, my dream job, my dream life, none of that meant anything to me anymore. My happiness was dependent on how well I played."[15]

OK, now Jeremy knew what he was dealing with. Stripped of everything else, he realized that even the happiness he derived from seeing his shots swish through the net, hearing "attaboys" from the coaches, and acknowledging explosive cheers from the fans is short-lived. The lesson learned is that success is fleeting, but that what really counts is an attitude of humble dependence on God.

Basketball had become an idol in Jeremy's life, and if he was dependent on making the game the source of his happiness, then he was destined to become one unhappy dude. He decided to trust God for his future, which gave him a whole new perspective on everything.

In our interviews, Jeremy and I had this exchange about the demotion:

How did you take those struggles, being sent down to D-League?

Jeremy: It was really hard. People don't believe me when I say it was the toughest year of my life, but it was. I had a lot of long nights and struggles and had to really learn how to submit my will to God and really learn to trust and just to go through different situations that I thought were maybe unfair at times or things I had wished would have gone a different way.

What I learned was to lean on God in those situations and to make my relationship more intimate, to develop my relationship, and to spend more time with him every day. A lot of different convictions were coming up, and I did a lot of reading, and I did a lot of praying. More praying than I had ever done. I just learned a ton.

The first time you got sent to Reno, was it a shock to you?

Jeremy: Yes, it was a shock because I did not realize how different the two leagues were. I had always heard about it, but not until you go there do you really realize how different they are. The first time I went down, that is when I started to realize—it was really humbling, when I realized that wow, you know in the NBA, I was complaining about this and complaining about that, and it gave me a whole new perspective on everything and gave me a little more sense of gratitude.

Some of the differences are what? The type of meal money you got? The type of hotel you stay at?

Jeremy: Just everything. Locker rooms, facilities, the attendance at the games, the service, everything. The travel. It's all very different.

Did you ever have to take a bus to a game?

Jeremy: It depends. Sometimes you take a bus, like the time we had a nine-hour bus ride to Bakersfield.

Being sent down to Reno was a trial, and James 1:2 promises believers that they will face adversities of many kinds. But it wasn't the end of the world—or the end of Jeremy's NBA aspirations. It was this knowledge that gave him a total attitude adjustment: if going down to D-League is what the Warriors wanted him to do, then that's what he would do. He would listen to his coaches, work on his weaknesses, and play hard.

One thing that didn't change about him was his servant's heart. For example, when the team traveled by air to places like Erie, New York; Canton, Ohio; and the border town of Hidalgo, Texas, Jeremy was entitled to roomier first-class seating since he was on assignment from the Warriors. The roster players were consigned to the cramped economy class—steerage. Wedging their six-foot, nine-inch bodies into their seats was a gymnastic trick worthy of a Cirque du Soleil production.

Jeremy always gave up his first-class ticket to a taller teammate and sat in the back of the plane. "That really spoke volumes about what type of guy he is," said Eric Musselman, his coach with the Reno Bighorns. "Our players loved playing with him."[16]

Jeremy played well in Reno, averaging in Reno, averaging 18 points, 5.6 rebounds, and 4.3 assists per game. He got both minutes and much-needed experience playing in a professional league.

He wasn't confident yet, but he was a lot more comfortable when he was on the court, and that showed in his improved play.

Jeremy Left His Heart in ... Reno

Following the rise of Linsanity, the Reno Bighorns front office knew a good promotion when they saw one. During a March 17, 2012, game, they had "Jeremy Lin Giveaway Night" and handed out 1,500 limited edition jerseys—even though Jeremy was no longer playing for the Golden State Warriors organization.

The jerseys went like proverbial hotcakes—and some became hot items on eBay.

The Tempting Life

There's no doubt that Jeremy discovered that playing in the NBA was not an easy gig. The long season had players bouncing from city to city like a pinball rolling down a slanted surface of pins and targets. The physical strain of playing on back-to-back nights in different cities fatigues the legs and zaps the desire to perform and play well. Even the best-conditioned athletes have to pace themselves during the season—even during games—so they have something in reserve for a fourth-quarter rally.

Besides the physical demands, I would argue that

Christian hoopsters like Jeremy have it even tougher in the NBA because of the temptations that bombard them daily. They are presented with every reason to turn their backs on Christ and rely on themselves as they seek fame and fortune in this world.

In their defense, NBA players face challenges and temptations that the rest of us can't even begin to understand. They have money; they have a lot of free time on their hands; they have flocks of women hoping to catch their eyes in hotel lobbies, restaurants, and bars. The ladies are dressed provocatively, are attractive, and flirt like schoolgirls with come-hither looks.

Some, unfortunately, are looking to get impregnated by an NBA player. They see having a child out of wedlock as a fast-track ticket to child support payments that begin in the five figures and can rise to sums of $75,000 a month. The number of illegitimate children of NBA players is staggering — and commonplace in other professional sports too — but it's generally estimated that 50 to 60 percent of all players have had children out of wedlock. Child support payments are some athletes' single largest expense.

One of the players I featured in my *Playing with Purpose* basketball book told me that the NBA once sent out a representative to talk to the players about "how to be careful."

"He basically told us how to cheat and get away with it," he said. "It was pretty crazy. He told us to get a prepaid cell phone that wasn't registered in our name and not to leave any phone or text messages. He informed us that if you have unprotected sex and knock up a girl, there are consequences, especially in New York City, where the state of New York will hit you with an alimony bill of $75,000 a month if you make the league average of $5 million. He urged us to take precautions because there are a lot of girls out there who are after your money."

Despite the threat of paternity suits, sexually transmitted diseases, or the emptiness associated with love-'em-and-leave-'em one-night stands, the easy availability of women sends many NBA players down a path "like an ox going to the slaughter, like a deer stepping into a noose," as the wisest man who ever lived, King Solomon, stated in Proverbs 7:22. That's why we need to be praying for those who are staying strong—the Jeremy Lins of today—as well as for those who can't seem to resist the lures of the world around them.

"Most people forget that we're talking about kids in their early twenties," said Jeff Ryan, the chaplain for the Orlando Magic. "If you can remember your early twenties—and I remember mine—you don't always make the right choices. I was fortunate that I didn't have the temptations that these guys have. Remember, they are targeted. Some handle it well, and some don't. Unfortunately, there are plenty of guys who get caught up in the women thing and get their heads turned. They come into the league with the best of intentions, wanting to be faithful, wanting to be strong, but they give in to temptation. It's like my doctor telling me what I shouldn't eat. Once in a while I'm going to have it anyway. I think that's what happens to a lot of these guys. They know they shouldn't, but they give in."

In our interviews, Jeremy told me that his mom and dad warned him about the temptations found in the NBA. "They said, 'Be smart. There are going to be girls throwing themselves at you, so be smart.' Typical parent stuff," Jeremy said. "They also reminded me to make sure that I took care of my relationship with God first."

"So was it difficult or easy being a Christian in the NBA?" I asked Jeremy after he finished his rookie season.

"I don't want to say it was easy, but it wasn't as bad as I thought it would be. It helped that I had a couple of teammates who were strong Christians — Stephen Curry and Reggie Williams. We would go to chapel together before the games and occasionally have conversations about our faith, so that was definitely helpful. I had a lot of accountability in terms of a small group at home. And I was at home playing for the Warriors, so I went to my home church whenever I could. I had my pastor, Stephen Chen, and then I had my small group."

Having his family nearby made the transition into the pros a lot easier, Jeremy told me, but the difficult part was not having any type of rhythm.

"You know, church is really tough to attend, and the schedule is so crazy. I had to listen to sermons on my computer on a lot of Sundays. The sermons would not always be from my home church but from a variety of places. My dad burned a bunch of sermons for me onto a CD, so I would carry a little case of all the sermons. Devotionals were a big part of my walk—just quiet times in my hotel rooms."

I asked Jeremy about those stretches in hotel rooms, since there's a lot of downtime in the NBA during long road trips that can stretch from five to eight days.

"Yeah, I had more spare time this year and more time to spend with God this year than I have ever had," he said. "That was one of the parts that made it easier compared to being in college, where you wake up, go to class, practice, then do your homework, and go to sleep. I had a lot more free time, since I was no longer in school."

"And what about the temptations?" I asked. "I imagine one of the difficulties about playing in the NBA is all the women who hang around the hotel rooms and all the people who try to talk to you and that type of thing."

"Yes, I think that's definitely true, but it wasn't really an issue for me because I didn't go out very much. And then there were guys on my team I hung out with, and we had a different lifestyle, so it wasn't a huge issue. It's definitely out there if you want it, but I chose to take it out of play. Once you take a stand for something at the beginning, everybody respects that, and they don't bother you about it."

Wrapping Up

After bouncing back and forth between Reno and Oakland, Jeremy finished the last two weeks of the season with the parent club and finished on a high note in the Warriors' final game in mid-April, scoring 12 points and playing 24 minutes in a win over the Portland Trail Blazers. When you tally up the totals, he had played in only twenty-nine games for a struggling Golden State team that finished 36–46.

So what was his assessment of his rookie season?

"People don't believe me when I say my rookie season was the toughest year of my life, but it was." Echoing words he had said to me when we talked about his demotion to Reno, he summarized the season: "I had to really learn how to submit my will to God and learn to trust him while going through situations I thought were maybe unfair or things I wished would have gone differently. I learned to lean on God and to spend more time with him every day. I did a lot of reading and a lot of praying, and through it I did a lot of growing."

Jeremy had signed a two-year contract with Golden State, so there was every expectation that the team would continue to bring him along, give him more playing time, and help him become the best player he could be.

Funny how things worked out.

Chapter 5

THE LOCKOUT

The 2011 NBA lockout was the fourth in the league's history and nearly cost the league the 2011–12 season. As it was, the 161-day work stoppage began on July 1, 2011, and ended on December 8, 2011. The lockout delayed the start of the regular season from November 1 to Christmas Day and reduced the regular season from 82 to 66 games.

During the lockout, Jeremy could not step inside the Warriors' gleaming training facility in downtown Oakland. Nor was he allowed any contact with the coaches, trainers, or staff. It was up to Jeremy to stay in shape, but he didn't lack in motivation and determination. He worked harder than ever to be ready when the NBA started up again.

His schedule was Navy SEAL Team 6 material:

- 10:00 to 11:00 a.m.: agility training
- 11:00 a.m. to noon: weight training

- 1:00 to 2:00 p.m.: shooting work with a private coach
- 2:00 to 4:00 p.m.: individual work[17]

He posted YouTube videos of his maniacal workouts on the court and in the weight room with trainer Phil Wagner. He got results. He nearly tripled the number of pull-ups (from 12 to 30), more than doubled the weight he could squat (from 110 pounds to 231 pounds), added 12 pounds of muscle to his 200-pound frame, and boosted his vertical leap by 3.5 inches.

He also worked on a hitch in his shooting form that dated back to eighth grade. Doc Scheppler, the girls basketball coach at Pinewood High School in Los Altos Hills, noticed that he brought the ball too far behind his head, which hurt his rhythm on his release. Scheppler taught him how to "load" his shot earlier and release the ball in rhythm at the apex of his jump. They practiced 90 minutes a day, 3 to 4 times a week, taking 500 to 600 shots each session.

"That's the lesson here," Scheppler said. "If you don't like the way things are going for you in a sport, don't cry about it. Don't whine to the coach. Do something about it."[18] In the process, Jeremy reinvented himself, shot by shot and pound by pound.

Meanwhile, he kept an eye on the latest news of the contract negotiations between the NBA owners and the players' union. As each "deadline" passed without an agreement, both sides inched closer to the unthinkable —the cancellation of the entire season.

At the eleventh hour, an agreement was reached on November 25, 2011. NBA commissioner David Stern announced that the first practice would be Friday, December 9, with the season officially beginning on Christmas Day.

Jeremy arrived at the Oakland facility for the first day of practice and suited up. He had just met his new coach, Mark Jackson, who had never seen him play. Undoubtedly, Jeremy felt mounting pressure to prove himself all over again.

He was loosening up when he was told that general manager Larry Riley wanted to see him. The Warriors hadn't even started their layup drills.

If you've seen the Brad Pitt movie *Moneyball*, you know it's never good news when the GM asks to see you. This occasion was no exception.

Jeremy, the Warriors organization has decided to put you on waivers. We think you'll clear the waiver wire so that we'll get you back.

No matter how much perfume Riley sprayed into the air, the pronouncement stunk. Jeremy was being let go, cut from the team, categorically released. For all he knew, his short-lived NBA career was over.

This is where the "business" side of professional basketball can turn a player's dream into a nightmare in a heartbeat. What happened was that the Golden State management made a calculated decision to go after Los Angeles Clipper center DeAndre Jordan, a restricted free agent, to shore up a big hole in the low post. But to make Jordan an offer he couldn't refuse, the Warriors had to create room under their salary cap. That meant moving a few pieces around the chessboard: cut Jeremy loose, use their amnesty clause on veteran guard Charlie Bell, and delay the signing of two rookies they liked—Klay Thompson and Jeremy Tyler. Then, under salary cap rules, the team would have enough money to bring in the center they desperately needed.

Once Jordan was signed, sealed, and delivered, the Warriors could bring Jeremy back—if no other team claimed him.

On the same day—December 9—something important to Jeremy's story was happening in New York. The Knicks waived veteran point guard Chauncey Billups and signed center Tyson Chandler, leaving the team out of cap space and without a true point guard.

Three days later, the Houston Rockets picked up Jeremy, so he couldn't go back to his childhood team. To add insult to injury, Clippers owner Donald Sterling—a notorious skinflint—matched Golden State's overly generous four-year, $43 million offer for DeAndre Jordan, which meant the bruising center was staying in Los Angeles.

Talk about collateral damage. Golden State's gamble had blown up in their faces, and Jeremy was starting all over in Houston with a new team.

Jeremy arrived in Space City to discover he would have to take a number and wait his turn to make an impression on the coaches. The Rockets were overstocked with point guards, and Jeremy had a hard time getting reps in practice. In two preseason games with the Rockets, he got on the floor for a total of just under 8 minutes.

"At the time, I was thinking if this doesn't work out, I maybe needed to take a break from basketball," Jeremy told Marcus Thompson II of the *San Jose Mercury News*. "I put in four months of training. I felt like I worked harder than anyone else. And now I was fighting for a chance to practice. I was questioning everything."[19]

Then, on Christmas Eve, Jeremy woke up to find a lump of coal under his tree: he was being waived—let go—by Houston. This time, general manager Daryl Morey was the bearer of bad news, and he didn't salve the wound by saying that he hoped Jeremy would be back. His explanation was that the Rockets needed cap room to sign Haitian center Samuel Dalembert.

Merry Christmas, kid. Best of luck to you.

This could have been the end of the line. Yet Jeremy knew that faith is "confidence in what we hope for and assurance about what we do not see" (Hebrews 11:1), and this latest zigzag was not the time to doubt that God was still in control. It was the time to double down on his commitment to the Lord.

"Lin headed back to the Bay Area defeated, but with a renewed purpose. He gave up trying to control everything," Thompson wrote. "He tried to stop worrying."

The day after Christmas, Jeremy woke up at his parents'

place and did a devotional before heading to the gym to stay in shape. During his shootaround, each time anxiety about the future crept in, he whispered Romans 8:28 to himself: "We know that in all things God works for the good of those who love him, who have been called according to his purpose."

Something good was about to happen—he was sure of it. But Jeremy had no idea that more trials were ahead of him.

New York, New York

The New York Knicks had a guard problem.

When the lockout was over, the club signed thirty-two-year-old Baron Davis to be their point guard, even though he had a back injury that would keep him out until late February. Until Davis could join the team, the Knicks would forge ahead with veteran guards Mike Bibby and Toney Douglas at point and Iman Shumpert as a shooting guard. Bill Walker (six foot six) and Landry Fields (six foot seven) were small forwards who could play in the backcourt too.

Then in the Christmas Day season opener against the Boston Celtics, Iman Shumpert got tangled up in the low post and injured his right knee. After the game, the team medical staff called the injury a sprained medial collateral ligament and said Shumpert would need two to four weeks to heal.

The Knicks were down to two guards.

John Gabriel, the director of pro scouting and free agency for the Knicks, said that every team looking for a point guard has a certain player in mind. "You want somebody who has good size. He can make the open shot and is getting better on defense. Leadership was looking for someone who would be good at running Mike's system," he told me, referring to head coach Mike D'Antoni. "That includes making shots, running the floor, being able to push the ball during transition, as well as defend. Those were desired key attributes."

Paging Magic Johnson.

Unfortunately, Magic wasn't available, and neither was Michael Jordan or Oscar Robertson. Knicks' interim general manager Glen Grunwald and his assistant GM Allan Houston searched the waiver wire for who was available — and Jeremy Lin's name was there.

Actually, Jeremy wasn't an unknown entity to the Knicks' front office staff. He had been on the Knicks' radar for some time after he made some noise at Harvard.

"We liked him," Grunwald said. "We worked him out in the draft. We had discussions with Golden State when he was there. It was just an opportunity to acquire him when we needed someone who had his skill set."[20]

What the Knicks' brain trust saw in the video breakdown of Jeremy was more athleticism than they thought. He was a good decision maker on when to go and not to go. He was worth the risk.

On December 27, the team claimed Jeremy off of waivers to fill a void at backup point guard, prompting Knicks' head coach Mike D'Antoni to say, "Yeah, we picked up Jeremy Lin off of waivers [as] a backup point [guard] in case. We've always liked him as a player, so we'll see where we go with it."

Reaction among the New York media was a bit muted. "The Knicks offense didn't get a huge boost Tuesday, but their collective GPA sure did," sniffed *New York Daily News* beat writer Sean Brennan, referring to the new Ivy Leaguer in their midst.[21]

Jeremy didn't see it that way. He updated his Twitter account with this message: "Thankful to God for the opportunity to be a New York Knick!! Time to find my winter coats from college lol!"

He was back in the NBA, but his contract wasn't guaranteed until February 10. Up until that date, he could be cut any day, so there was no reason to shop for a Fifth Avenue penthouse.

Fortunately, by this time his big brother Josh was living in Manhattan, attending New York University as a dental student. Josh and his wife, Patricia, had set up housekeeping in a one-bedroom apartment on the Lower East Side, so if Jeremy didn't mind sleeping on the couch...

In those early days, he had to do some fast-talking each time he approached the player entrance before home games. "Everytime i try to get into Madison Square Garden, the security guards ask me if im a trainer LOL," he tweeted.[22]

The Rising Tide of Social Media

Since he's a millennial who grew up in Silicon Valley with parents in high-tech jobs in the computer industry, Jeremy has been an early adopter of technology. He's been posting his own videos on YouTube since his college days at Harvard and has more than 200,000 subscribers to TheJLin7, his official channel on YouTube. The YouTube videos I checked out were engaging, interesting, and even hilarious; most were day-in-the-life "episodes" of working out, meeting fans, traveling to Taiwan — and sneaking out from his hotel to play late-night hoops with the locals — and interactions with friends.

He taps out tweets three or four times a week to his nearly one million followers on Twitter. He gets it when it comes to the use of social media. His Twitter avatar shows an illustration of a white-robed Christ sitting on a bench with a young man in a pastoral scene. A large duffel bag and sleeping bag are on the ground next to the bench, implying that the young man may be homeless. The meaningful caption underneath the illustration reads as follows: "No, I'm not talking about Twitter. I literally want you to follow me" — Jesus.[23]

You can follow Jeremy on Twitter at @JLin7 (his current number with the Houston Rockets).

Jeremy was parked at the end of the bench like there was a wheel clamp strapped to his Nikes. D'Antoni rarely called his number, which was No. 17. His favorite, No. 7, wasn't available because the team's marquee player, Carmelo Anthony, had already claimed it. During a press conference at the NBA All-Star weekend, Jeremy said he chose 17 because the number 1 represented himself and the number 7 represented God. "When I went to D-League, I had 17, and so everywhere I go, [God] would be right there next to me. And so that's why I stuck with 17."[24]

From December 28 to January 16, Jeremy played 16 minutes in 12 games, scoring a total of 9 points. Since the Knicks were losing more than they were winning, there was no way Jeremy could get into the offensive flow in the waning minutes of the game, when the outcome had been decided and the play was chaotic and unrehearsed. He couldn't learn D'Antoni's system because very few practice days could be scheduled in the contracted season.

On January 17, Jeremy was demoted to D-League—the Erie BayHawks, the Knicks' developmental team affiliate.

Not again!

About this turn of events, Jeremy said, "I had no opportunity to prove myself. There was definitely a little bit of 'What's going on?' in my prayers. My flesh was constantly pulling at me. Whine. Complain. Whine. Complain. But the other side of me was thinking, *My God is all-powerful* ... When I look back, there are so many times in my life where I've questioned God. Why do I even doubt God? At the same time, it's a growing process."[25]

And at least Jeremy would get to play ball. In his Bay-

Hawks debut against the Maine Red Claws on January 20, Jeremy laid down a triple double—28 points, 12 assists, and 11 rebounds. He played 45 of the 48 minutes and repeatedly beat defenders with an extremely quick first step.

The Knicks scouts were impressed, as they should have been. Jeremy was immediately recalled to New York, where the season was going nowhere fast. Throughout the rest of January and early February, losses piled up like snowdrifts. Six losses in a row. Win a game. Three losses in a row.

Mike Bibby and Toney Douglas were playing poorly. Baron Davis was still out. Iman Shumpert showed little aptitude for the point guard position. Then Carmelo Anthony, the team's leading scorer, suffered a groin injury in mid-January and looked to be out for six weeks. There was no clear ball handler or offensive catalyst on the Knicks. Jeremy was still the forgotten man on the bench.

On Saturday, February 4, at halftime of a home game against the New Jersey Nets, the injured star Carmelo Anthony—dressed in street clothes—pulled Coach D'Antoni aside in the locker room and suggested he play Jeremy more. See what the kid could do. What was there to lose? The Knicks had been beaten in five of their previous six games and were on a 2–11 losing jag.

Jeremy played like he was back with the Erie BayHawks —aggressively, like he belonged in the NBA. D'Antoni left him in, and Jeremy grabbed the reins of leadership. He scored 25 points, snared 5 rebounds, and dished out 7 assists—all career highs—in leading the Knicks to a 99–92 victory.

D'Antoni liked what he saw—a real point guard running the offensive show. "You're starting Monday night," he told the second-year player.

Linsanity was about to be unleashed on an unsuspecting public.

Chapter 6

THE MIRACLE NEAR
34TH STREET

On the morning of Jeremy's first NBA start against the Utah Jazz on Monday, February 6, the Knicks' webmaster made some changes to the team's website. The smiling face of youthful Jeremy Lin greeted eyeballs on the splash page. The marketing department sent out an e-blast with "Linsanity!" in the subject line.

The Knicks were shorthanded without Amar'e Stoudemire, who was granted bereavement leave after his older brother, Hazell, was killed in a car crash in Florida. Carmelo Anthony tried to play but had to leave the game after six minutes because of a strained right groin.

Time to step up.

Jeremy set the tempo again with dazzling dribbling and sweet drives to the basket. A nifty midair hand change for a reverse layup prompted the Knicks' home crowd to chant "MVP! MVP!" They were obviously still in a celebratory mood after cheering their beloved New York Giants to a come-from-behind victory over the New England Patriots a day before in Super Bowl XLVI.

Jeremy scored a career-high 28 points against Utah, showing that his 25-point performance against the New Jersey Nets was no fluke. The fact that Jeremy orchestrated a win against a decent team attracted some notice around the league. But this was going to be a busy week for the Knicks. On Wednesday, they had a quick road trip to play the Washington Wizards, then a return home to host the Kobe-led Lakers on Friday night, followed by another road trip to Minnesota to play the T-Wolves on Saturday night.

No Blues in This Guy

A Facebook page titled "Jeremy Lin's Blue Tongue" was launched after NBA TV cameras caught him sticking out his tongue — in exhilaration — toward the end of the win over Utah Jazz. There it was — a blue streak on the fleshy muscular organ in his mouth.

It leads me to wonder if cases of Gatorade G2 Blueberry-Pomegranate Thirst Quencher started flying off the shelves.

Awaiting Jeremy in the nation's capital was John Wall. Remember him? He was the No. 1 pick in the 2010 draft — and Jeremy's foil in the final game of Summer League,

One-year-old Jeremy is held in the arms of his father, Gie-Ming, on this outing with his older brother, Josh, and his grandmother, Lin Chu A-muen.

Lin Chu A-muen, the mother of Gie-Ming, came over from Taiwan to help raise the family during Jeremy's formative years.

When Jeremy entered Palo Alto High as a five-foot-three freshman, his goal was to reach six feet in height so he would be a competitive basketball player.

Image provided by Josie Lepe/MCT/Landov

With a quick first step, Jeremy drives past a defender in this high school basketball game. Jeremy led Palo Alto High to a California state championship his senior year.

Image provided by Dai Sugano/MCT/Landov

Jeremy put the Harvard basketball program on the map, leading the team to a 21-8 record his senior year.

Image provided by AP Photo/Nick Wass

Jeremy's big break came during the final game of the July 2010 NBA Summer League, when he outplayed, outhustled, and outshone his opponents, impressing NBA scouts.

Image provided by Garrett W. Ellwood/NBAE via Getty Images

Jeremy was all smiles with his parents, Shirley and Gie-Ming, when he signed a two-year contract in the summer of 2010 to play for his hometown team, the Golden State Warriors.

Image provided by Paul Sakuma/AP Images

In Golden State's second home game of the 2010-2011 season on "Asian Heritage Night," 17,408 fans exploded with cheers when Jeremy played his first minutes in the NBA. He would go on to warm the bench and play in only 29 games for the Warriors and was sent three times to the Reno Bighorns, the Warriors' D-League affiliate, to work on his game and get some playing time.

Jeremy shakes hands with recently retired Houston Rockets center Yao Ming of China during a charity basketball game in Taipei, Taiwan. Jeremy scored 17 points while playing with other NBA players on "Team Love."

Image provided by Wu Ching-Teng/Xinhua/Landov

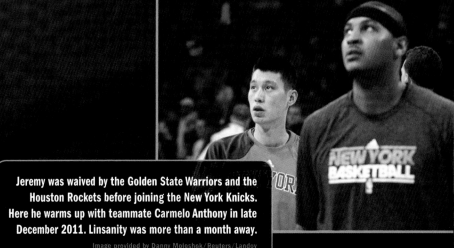

Jeremy was waived by the Golden State Warriors and the Houston Rockets before joining the New York Knicks. Here he warms up with teammate Carmelo Anthony in late December 2011. Linsanity was more than a month away.

Image provided by Danny Moloshok/Reuters/Landov

The Knicks had lost 2 of its last 13 games when star player Carmelo Anthony suggested to head coach Mike D'Antoni that he put Jeremy into the game against the New Jersey Nets on February 4, 2012. Jeremy led the Knicks to victory, scoring 25 points off the bench, and was named a starter, setting off Linsanity.

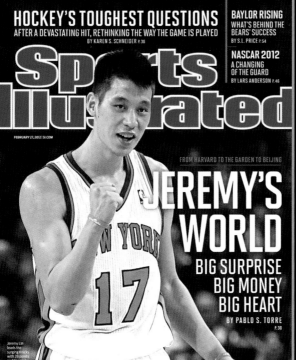

Top image provided by SI Cover/*Sports Illustrated*/Getty Images

How rare is that double? Since 1990, only 11 other athletes have graced the cover of *Sports Illustrated*, the country's premier sports magazine, for two consecutive weeks.

Bottom image provided by Heinz Kluetmeier/*Sports Illustrated*/Getty Images

Jeremy makes a slashing move on the Miami Heat's LeBron James. One of the first things Jeremy did after joining the Rockets was ask for No. 7 — the biblical number denoting completeness or perfection — as his jersey number. Jeremy wore No. 7 during his rookie year at Golden State.

Image provided by Pat Sullivan/AP Images

A joyful Jeremy points heavenward after nailing a 3-pointer to lift the Knicks over the Raptors on February 14, 2012. Notice his wristband, which reads, "In Jesus' Name I Play."

Image provided by Frank Gunn/
The Canadian Press/AP Images

Taiwanese fans gather to watch Jeremy play basketball. Many Americans don't realize how popular Jeremy is in the Asian culture, who see him as one of their own.

Image provided by Wally Santana/AP Images

the game where Jeremy played flawlessly and earned a roster spot with the Golden State Warriors.

On this evening, Jeremy was being guarded closely by Wall when he employed a crossover dribble and blew past the defender like his sneakers were nailed to the floor. The lane opened up like the parting of the Red Sea. Instead of kissing the ball off the glass with a layin, Jeremy elevated and threw down a one-handed dunk that even excited the Wizards' home crowd.

"I think they messed up their coverage," Jeremy said after the game.[26]

Chalk up Jeremy's first double-double—23 points and 10 assists in a 107–93 victory.

A tsunami was building. It wouldn't crest yet. That would happen two days later when Kobe and the Lakers came to the Garden. But for now, "the fluke no longer looks so flukey," wrote Howard Beck in the *New York Times*. "The aberration is not fading away. Jeremy Lin is not regressing to the mean, whatever that mean is supposed to be."[27]

Midterm Exam

And then the Los Angeles Lakers rolled into the Big Apple for a Friday night game that sizzled with anticipation.

Here were two storied franchises from the nation's top two most populous cities squaring off, and the story line of Jeremy versus Kobe was too great to pass up for the dozens of scribes and TV news producers covering the Knicks beat.

After lighting the fuse on Linsanity, surely Jeremy would be put in his place by the great Kobe Bryant. Surely the thirty-three-year-old Lakers star had taken notice of Linsanity and would show this young buck a thing or two. Surely Jeremy wasn't still sleeping on his brother's couch.

Actually, he wasn't. Now he was sleeping on the couch of his teammate Landry Fields. The night before his breakout game against the New Jersey Nets, Jeremy found himself homeless. The comfy sofa on which he laid his head at his brother and sister-in-law's pad on the Lower East Side was reserved for friends coming over for a party.

Landry heard about Jeremy's plight and said he could crash at his place in White Plains, New York, which was close to the Knicks' training facility. Landry had a nice large brown couch in the living room. A flat-screen TV, refrigerator, and bathroom were steps away. What more did a bachelor need?

Once the Knicks got hot, there was no way that Jeremy or Landry were going to change a winning routine. Jeremy was sleeping on that couch, whether he wanted to or not.

And now a date loomed with Kobe Bryant—the player Jeremy shared a birthday with—in the heart of downtown Manhattan. It's hard to describe how the American and global media apparatus had trained its lens on Madison Square Garden that evening, but they had. A galaxy of celebrities was on hand, including filmmaker and Knicks superfan Spike Lee, actor Ben Stiller, erstwhile wrestler and actor Dwayne "The Rock" Johnson, and New York Giants defensive end Justin Tuck.

A lot—really a lot—was riding on the sinewy shoulders of Jeremy Shu-How Lin. He had everything to gain and much to lose, which is why you have to love what he did that night. All the pressure, all the hype, all the microphones, all the cameras examining every muscle twitch—and Jeremy didn't flinch.

I mean, laying down 38 points on Kobe and the Lakers was ridiculous. He made everything, including scoring 9 of the team's first 13 points to help the Knicks build a large lead. Analysts like to call that "making a statement." He nailed short jumpers, put a deft spin move on Derek Fisher to beat him to the hoop, and flung in a 3-pointer from the left baseline. Kobe nearly matched him, scoring 24 of his 34 points in the second half—but Bryant left the Garden on the wrong side of a 92–85 Knicks victory.

There was a telling moment when the torch of popularity may have been passed. Derek Fisher had been guarding Jeremy, but on this possession, Kobe and Jeremy were running down the court together. Kobe reached out and put his hand on Jeremy's body. This was a subtle yet effective way for Kobe to establish defensive dominance and put Jeremy in a subservient position.

Jeremy, without hesitation, quickly but firmly pushed the hand away, as if to say, *There's a new sheriff in town.*

Jeremy proved he was no one-week wonder in outplaying Kobe Bryant and the Lakers team. He was being called the "Taiwanese Tebow" — a paean to quarterback Tim Tebow's amazing 2012 season that lifted the Denver Broncos back into the NFL playoffs — for the way he impacted his teammates, lifted their games, and spoke forthrightly and earnestly about his faith.

The hype surrounding Jeremy would only grow. He was legit. The guy was for real. With the victory over the Lakers, he had four straight games with at least 20 points and 7 assists. In the history of the NBA — since the 1976 NBA/ABA merger — no player had scored more points in his first four starts.

More importantly, Jeremy had embraced the challenge of beating one of the league's top franchises in his first nationally televised game.

A Life of Its Own

With Kobe and the Lakers sent packing, New Yorkers couldn't stop talking about Jeremy Lin, and headline writers couldn't help themselves.

Gentlemen, start your puns.

The headlines ranged from the good to the bad to the pathetic:

- "Linsightful Lessons of Linsanity" (Huffington Post)

- "American-Born Linderella Is Pride of China" (NPR)

- "Just Lin Time: Knicks Phenom Saving Season" (*Chicago Tribune*)

- "Never Lin-visible, Knicks Sensation Just Needed a Chance" (*San Diego Union-Tribune*)

- "New York Knicks Legend Willis Reed Gives Ringing Lin-dorsement" (ESPN)

- "Linternational House of Fancakes" (sbnation.com)

- "Is Super Lintendo All-Hype or the Real Deal?" (The Renegade Rip)

Linsanity even invaded the Sunday morning pulpit. The Rev. John Lin—who was no relation but was kidded nonetheless about sharing the same last name of New York's favorite son—began his sermon at Redeemer Presbyterian on East 68th by announcing he would be teaching out of Matthew 1 about the incarnation.

"Or if you're a Knicks fan, you can call it the Lincarnation," he quipped.[28]

And that was the tip of the proverbial iceberg. Since there are twenty-seven pages of words that start with the prefix *in-* in my *American Heritage Dictionary*, and I count an average of forty words per page, this means you have approximately 1,080 combinations to choose from if you want to have some fun with *Lin*.

"I didn't know you could turn *Lin* into so many things, because we've never done it before," Jeremy told Kevin Armstrong of the *New York Daily News*. "Me and my family just laugh. I guess we underestimated how creative people can be."[29]

Live from New York, It's Saturday Night!

You know you're sitting atop the fulcrum of pop culture when *Saturday Night Live* does a hilarious skit about you, and that was the case for Jeremy as he turned Manhattan on its head:

Announcer No. 1 (playing it straight): From the set of "New York Sports Now," I'm Dan Mardell for our special report on Knicks point guard Jeremy Lin and the Linsanity surrounding him. Despite the Knicks' loss to New Orleans, the Big Apple is still in the middle of a Jeremy Lin Linvasion. Fellas, do you have Linsanity?

Announcer No. 2 (excited): You better lock me up. I am criminally Linsane!

Announcer No. 3 (really excited): My feelings are Lintense!

Announcer No. 4 (over-the-top excited): It's Lindescribable! I mean, I'm literally lin love with this Jeremy Lin!

Announcer No. 1 (playing it straight): I agree that we'll never get tired of Lin puns.

Announcer No. 4 (once more, but still over the top): As Charlie Sheen would say, *Linning!*[30]

A New Pregame Ritual

The Knicks had a tall order following their win over the Lakers: hop on the team plane and fly to Minneapolis for a game the following night. Prior to tip-off, Jeremy and his "roommate" Landry Fields enacted a rather unique pregame ritual that they had tried out against the Washington Wizards four days earlier.

Facing each other in front of the Knicks' bench, Jeremy pretended to flip through an imaginary book that Landry was holding in his hands. Then the pair pretended to take off their reading glasses, which they placed into imaginary pocket protectors. The routine ended with both players simultaneously pointing to the heavens and giving each other a pat on the backside.

OK, so it wasn't as dramatic as LeBron James tossing talcum powder into the air, but it was pretty cute. More than a few bloggers figured it had to be some sort of nerdy, bookworm faux handshake involving a Harvard grad with a former Stanford student-athlete. Actually, there was a lot more significance to it than that.

Landry Fields said that after Jeremy's first start, they had to come up with something since everyone was talking about the Harvard/Stanford connection between the two. "So we wanted to go out there and do something that was lighthearted and not too serious," he said.

The book is not a college textbook, Landry said, but God's Word. "It's a Bible because at the end of the day, that's what we're playing for. And that's why we point up toward the sky at the end."[31] (You can watch Jeremy and Landry break down their "secret" handshake on Jeremy's TheJLin7 official YouTube channel.)

The Jeremy Lin Show, meanwhile, played well off Broadway. Jeremy scored 20 points, reaching the 20-point plateau for the fifth game in a row, and his free throw with 4.9 seconds left (after missing the first) gave the Knicks a 99–98 lead and capped a furious fourth-quarter 12–4 comeback run.

Jeremy and the Knicks team knew they had stolen one in Minnesota. After Jeremy started off hot in the first half with 15 points, the man guarding him, Ricky Rubio, showed why he was the league leader in steals. He forced Jeremy into making multiple turnovers, and Rubio even swatted away one of his layup attempts.

But just like there are no ugly babies, there is no such thing as an ugly win. The Knicks had now captured their fifth in a row without Carmelo Anthony and Amar'e Stoudemire, who was still with family in Florida for the funeral of his brother.

From my home in Southern California, I was doing my best to keep up with Linsanity. The Knicks, I noticed, finally got a breather—two glorious days—before their next game in Toronto against the Raptors.

The game wasn't on any of my 500 channels, so I did the next best thing: I turned to *NBA Gametime Live* late in the fourth quarter.

"Here's what's going on in Toronto," host Ernie Johnson said, who then showed a clip of Jeremy driving into the maw of the Raptor defense. Jeremy was met in the lane by Raptor Amir Johnson. A collision ensued, and on the continuation, Jeremy double-pumped a feathery four-footer into the hole before tumbling to the floor. Three-point play!

Jeremy's fearless drive to the rack capped a furious 17-point rally to tie the game. A minute and five seconds were left to play.

Great, I thought. *I'm just in time to see a thrilling ending.*

"We cannot take you live to that game because of contractual restrictions," Ernie said, as if he were reading my mind. "But we will keep you up to speed. It's 87 apiece in Toronto."

Ernie attempted to make small talk with analysts Greg Anthony and Chris Webber, but Anthony stared off into the distance, no doubt watching the live feed on an off-camera monitor.

Ten or fifteen seconds passed before Ernie interrupted the patter to announce an update from Toronto that they could show. The visual is still imprinted on my brain: Jeremy, yo-yoing the ball above the top of the key, letting the clock run down. The crowd of 20,000 on its feet. A quick feint, and Jeremy pulls up for a beyond-the-arc, high-flying rainbow that sails cleanly through the net to give the Knicks a 90–87 lead with .05 seconds to go.

"Are you kidding me?" E.J. exclaimed. "Are you kidding

me? This story gets crazier and crazier every night the Knicks play."

Jeremy had done it again, but what some commentators overlooked was the fact that Coach Mike D'Antoni had not called for a time-out after the Knicks snared an offensive rebound with 10 seconds to play.

Instead, D'Antoni left the ball in Jeremy's hands. The Raptors were on their heels, having seen a huge lead disappear, and the New York coach rightly recognized that all the momentum was with his guys. Total trust—he left the ball in Jeremy's hands.

And then Jeremy delivered the dagger to the Raptors' hearts.

Everybody Got on Board Quickly

Seats on the Jeremy Lin bandwagon were filling up rather quickly. Whoopi Goldberg proudly donned a white home team No. 17 Knicks jersey on the morning talkfest *The View*. Sarah Palin, during a stop in New York City, purchased a blue Linsanity T-shirt, which she held up for photographers. Donald Trump, when asked about Jeremy on *Access Hollywood*, pronounced that Jeremy was the real deal and great for New York. Singer Nicki Minaj said she was looking forward to hanging out with the Lin One during the All-Star weekend. (I don't think that happened.)

The Hoopster-in-Chief said he had been keeping tabs on Jeremy since "way back when."

"I knew about Jeremy before you did, or everybody else did," President Barack Obama told sports columnist Bill Simmons. Obama explained that U.S. Education Secretary Arne Duncan, who played basketball at Harvard, tipped him off while Jeremy was filling it up for the Crimson during Jeremy's senior year. "So I've been on the Jeremy Lin bandwagon for a while," said the president.[32]

San Francisco columnist William Wong took notice of all the love flowing toward Jeremy from both sides of the political aisle. "If he can unite Democrat Obama and right-wing Republicans like Trump and Palin, hey, maybe the kid has otherworldly powers that should be explored," he wrote.[33]

It seemed like everyone had something to say about Jeremy. Here is a sampling of some of the best quotes I've seen:[34]

"If you peel back the layers, the guy is an excellent story. He's got all the requisite skills to do well on the basketball floor. But hard work and perseverance are at the core here in terms of what he's taken advantage of. Here's a guy who labored, being ready at the right time, and he's capitalized fully on it."

> **James Brown**, CBS Sports analyst, former basketball player and captain at Harvard University, who is involved in youth ministry and is a longtime supporter of the Fellowship of Christian Athletes

"Jeremy Lin is now living this creative contradiction. Much of the anger that arises when religion mixes with sport or with politics comes from people who want to deny that this contradiction exists and who want to live in a world in which there is only one morality, one set of qualities and where everything is easy, untragic and clean. Life and religion are more complicated than that."

David Brooks, *New York Times* columnist

"The thing that comes to mind is the movie *Chariots of Fire*. So what I see when I see Lin is somebody who embodies that kind of spirit. When he plays basketball, there's this way that he feels pleasure, feels God's pleasure. It's not for any other purpose."

Christine Folch, New York City resident and Harvard University graduate

"What makes him real is that this guy can play basketball. He loves to compete. He loves the challenge."

Earvin "Magic" Johnson, Hall of Famer and former point guard for the Los Angeles Lakers

"In a world of infinite data and endless observation, Jeremy Lin has now broadsided us like an unseen torpedo, fired from a submarine we didn't even know existed."

Bryan Harvey, sports blogger

"Of all the drives, dunks, and dazzling shots Jeremy Lin is forcing upon the stars of the NBA, none of it compares with the moves he's putting on a larger collection of everyday people. Jeremy Lin has dribbled America into the previously quiet corner of its casual prejudice and lazy stereotypes of Asian-Americans."

> **Bill Plaschke,** sports columnist for the *Los Angeles Times*

"I was kind of salty at him for putting me in my place, but we're having fun with it. I'm a part of Linsanity."

> **Stephen Curry,** Golden State Warriors guard and former teammate of Jeremy Lin

Chapter 7

LEADERSHIP WRITTEN ALL OVER HIM

While Jeremy was in Toronto, I received a phone call from Pat Williams, the senior vice president of the Orlando Magic. Since Pat came into the NBA in 1968, he has been the general manager of four NBA teams and has written seventy-five books, mainly on the topics of leadership, teamwork, good business practices, being a better parent, and living a successful and rewarding life.

He has also carved out a successful career as one of America's top motivational and inspirational speakers, speaking 150 times a year to Fortune 500 companies such as Allstate, American Express, Disney, Nike, and Tyson Foods, as well as to national associations and nonprofit organizations. Pat had been a huge help to me with *Playing with Purpose*, opening doors and offering insights on what the National Basketball Association and many of the players were like.

During our conversation, Pat told me that during his

forty-four-year career with the NBA, he thought he'd seen it all—until the arrival of Linsanity.

"I don't remember anything happening quite like this before," he said. "You know, a player undrafted from the Ivy League, of all places. Gets cut a couple of times, and then out of desperation, with the Knicks floundering terribly, everything going down the tubes, they throw him into the game. And the next thing you know, he embarks on a five-game rant that the league has never seen before. It's just an amazing story. Unprecedented, really."

I asked Pat to put on his general manager hat and lay out a scouting report. "He's good," he began. "If you look at him, he's big at six foot three and 200 pounds. He has some great quickness and intelligence, obviously. He understands the game, sees the big picture. Teams now know you've got to really pay attention to him. He's no longer a secret. He seems comfortable in his own skin spiritually. I think he has an infectious faith, and it's real. That's my sense."

But what really caught Pat's trained eye was something he has written and spoken about to millions of people over the years—leadership. It is Pat's belief that the best leaders not only have vision, communicate well, have great relational skills, exhibit strong character, and act boldly, but they also pursue their roles, not for power, but to serve.

Jeremy Lin, he said, had all of these attributes in spades.

"Here is this kid who has been batted around as a

young pro basketball player, trying to make it on the big stage, and he comes into New York, and when he gets his chance, he takes the team over. It's like he said, *I am your leader! You have been waiting for me, and I am going to lead.* Usually players like this are very sensitive and timid. They wait their turn, and maybe five years later, when they feel more accepted, they'll step up and lead, but this kid seems to have leadership written all over him. And he isn't afraid to demonstrate it."

Pat said that coaches long to see leadership exhibited both on the floor and in the locker room. Many fans are unaware that issues crop up among teammates, if for no other reason than they see each other every single day for months at a time and can get on each other's nerves. Since people are people, even in the NBA world, irritations, slights, and constant teasing can result in angry words, dirty looks, and disunity.

"Coaches can't get down in the trenches with these sorts of things, so the guys who can clean up a lot of this stuff in the locker room are invaluable to a team," Pat pointed out. "That was Michael Jordan's great strength. He wasn't just a great player, but he was also a great leader. His coach in Chicago, Phil Jackson, never had to deal with a lot of these issues because they never got to him. Michael would get them resolved. I think we'll see the same thing with Jeremy because this guy doesn't look like he's afraid to lead."

John Gabriel, the Knicks' director of pro scouting and free agency and Pat's coworker for eighteen seasons with the Orlando Magic, said not every great player is a great leader. "I think, number one, that Jeremy has the confidence and the ability to articulate what he sees on the court and communicate it to his teammates and with the coaches. Remember, he's a rookie for the most part, and yet he's shown he has natural leadership qualities, a desired attribute that can take many years to develop," Gabriel said.

"I think Jeremy's philosophy is quite simple: *How can I help us win this game?*" Gabriel continued. "From there, he

Where Are the Tats?

You know what I find to be one of the most interesting things about Jeremy Lin? The fact that he doesn't have any tattoos. (If he does have any, they would have to be on skin covered by his team shorts.)

It almost seems you have to get inked up to join the NBA players union these days. Tattoos fill fleshy biceps, cover the back, occupy the chest, and run up and down the arms, wrists, and legs of just about every player in the league. But Jeremy's skin appears to be a tattoo-free zone, which is refreshing.

I get it that tattoos are cool and a way of making a statement about what's important to you. But the last time I checked, tats are permanent, which means they'll remain on your skin until the day you die. Sure, you can get them removed with painful laser treatments, but your skin is never the same after these procedures.

does whatever he needs to every time he crosses the half-court line. If that means taking and making big shots, he can and he will. But his strongest contribution may be seen in his desire to get others engaged and involved, an attribute felt by every player on our team and witnessed by so many who have enjoyed watching him play.

"He's making shots, which is a major component of our team's offense, and our coaching staff does a great job of instilling confidence in players. If you're on the court with Jeremy Lin and you're open, trust that he will find you."

Can you have a tattoo and still be a Christian? Of course you can. But players seem to forget that life changes. You grow out of your tats. You move on. What's popular now will be old, old news in five or ten years.

So, it seems that Jeremy is taking the long view. It's like comedian Sebastian Maniscalco's line in a recent performance: "Why would you put a bumper sticker on a Ferrari?"

Jeremy does make a "body" statement, however, with the sports wristbands he wears that are manufactured by a Christian company called Active Faith founded by former NBA player Lanny Smith and current Atlanta Hawks forward Anthony Toliver. Jeremy's rubber wristbands, which cost $3, read, **In Jesus' Name I Play.**

Now *that's* a great message — a pretty good bumper sticker, if you will. And Jeremy can take them off any time he wants.

Risk-Reward Basketball

Throughout February and leading up to the 2012 All-Star Game in Orlando, Florida, Jeremy continued to play at a high level. He logged a lot of minutes—37.6 minutes over the course of the twelve games—and averaged 22.5 points per game.

If analysts had a bone to pick with Jeremy's play, it was his turnovers, committing an eyebrow-raising 68 TOs in that twelve-game stretch—an average of 5.6 per game.

The Knicks' seven-game win streak that marked the start of Linsanity was snapped against the New Orleans Hornets when Jeremy struggled to protect the ball and connect with passes. Eight first-half turnovers—and poor team shooting—put the Knicks in a hole they couldn't overcome, despite a team-high 28 points, 5 assists, and 4 steals from Jeremy.

Jeremy owned up to what happened on the floor. *My bad.* But he did clean things up in the second half by turning the ball over only once.

"It was just a lackluster effort on my part coming out and [being] careless with the ball," he said after the game. "Nine turnovers is obviously never going to get it done from your primary ball handler. It's on me in terms of taking care of the ball, and also the game in general."[35]

He also had a couple of "snowmen" on the stat card —8 turnovers in the memorable Toronto Raptors' victory and an ugly 8 against the Miami Heat, when a swarming defense turned up the heat in the forecourt.

A turnover can happen in a variety of ways—the ball is stolen by the opponent, either through stripping away the ball off the dribble or intercepting a pass; a player can mistime a cutting teammate and throw the ball out of bounds, travel with the ball, or commit an offensive foul. Turnovers drive coaches crazy because they are often mental mistakes stemming from a lack of concentration. When the opposing team takes the ball back down the floor and scores quickly, that's often known as a "four-point switch" on the scoreboard. Instead of your team picking up two points, the other team scores a deuce.

Point guards are especially susceptible to committing turnovers, if for no other reason than that the transitional offense and set pieces both start with the ball in their hands probably 80 percent of the time. It's rare for a point guard to go an entire game without making a turnover. Coaches are more forgiving of aggressive turnovers —turnovers made when a guard drives fearlessly into the lane to make a play—because he is trying to create a play, to make something happen. Passive turnovers caused by a tentative player—the product of hesitation or uncertainty —are not viewed so kindly.

Jeremy's turnovers have generally been of the aggressive variety. When Jeremy dribbles the ball past the half-court line, he's looking to create something new. This may mean working the pick-and-roll with one of the forwards, advancing toward the top of key and tossing an alley-oop pass to a streaking teammate for a slam dunk, or drawing a double-team off the right side and hitting the off guard for an open look at a 3-point shot in the corner.

But his greatest attribute is his penetration into the lane, where things can get, well, crowded. Three players often collapse on him, and in the tangle of taller, more muscular arms grabbing at the ball, they will sometimes pry the ball away from him.

Turnover.

Forays into the lane are risk-reward efforts. More often than not good things happen—Jeremy either floats in a one-hander or kicks the ball out to one of his open teammates on the wings. This type of penetration is why the Knicks won so many games prior to the All-Star break, when Jerry took the team on a 9–3 run.

To counter this line of attack, opponents began springing a double-team on Jeremy as soon as he crossed the half-court stripe. Their goal was to disrupt the Knicks' offensive flow and push Jeremy into one of the corners near half-court, where they could trap him. With two large guys hounding him, passes to teammates could be intercepted. But if Jeremy could get the ball to an open teammate, the Knicks usually had a three-on-two break for the basket.

Some clubs tried to stop Jeremy by "jumping" the pick-and-roll or applying relentless defensive pressure to take away his passing lanes. A case in point was when the star-studded Miami Heat team, sporting the league's best record, put the clamps on Linsanity just before the All-

Star break—8 turnovers, 1 for 11 from the floor, and only 3 assists. The Heat did a great job of making Jeremy feel uncomfortable on the floor.

"They were all geeked up for him," Knicks' coach Mike D'Antoni said after the game. "They took the challenge and did a great job. It's hard to be Peter Pan every day."[36]

The All-Star Break

Jeremy stayed in the state of Florida following the Miami Heat game because he was a last-second addition to the NBA's Rising Stars Challenge, a game that was played two nights before the All-Star game. A pool of eighteen players had been selected before Linsanity, but NBA Commissioner David Stern—with a wet finger raised into the wind—called an audible and added Jeremy to the roster of players just before "coaches" Shaquille O'Neal and Charles Barkley began drafting their teams.

Shaq grabbed Jeremy after selecting monster dunker Blake Griffin of the Los Angeles Clippers as his first pick. The Rising Stars game was a supercasual lark, about as serious as an after-practice shootaround. Jeremy played a handful of minutes during the exhibition, which was an evening when defense took the night off. Jeremy scored one basket, but he did a great job not expending any energy. After back-to-back games, he needed a break.

Jeremy was supposed to be part of the 2012 Sprite Slam Dunk contest the following night, where the NBA's best elevators play a dunkathon version of "Can You Top This?" Blake "The Quake" Griffin won the Slam Dunk event the year before when he leaped over a Kia Optima SX parked in the three-second lane. After taking an alley-oop pass from Baron Davis, who was peeking out through the sunroof of the Kia—a choir singing R. Kelly's "I Believe I Can Fly" in the background—Griffin slammed home another of his patented one-handed monster jams. (And now you know why Blake Griffin is starring in those Kia car commercials in regular rotation these days.)

For the 2012 Slam Dunk contest, Jeremy wasn't going to attempt any acrobatic dunks himself, but his teammate Iman Shumpert had been toying with an idea. Teammate Landry Fields would roll into the three-second lane a large brown couch covered with a white sheet. Jeremy would be "sleeping" underneath the sheet. Then at the right moment, Landry would pull off the cover, and Jeremy would pop up and toss an alley-oop to Iman, who would jump over the couch on his way to the rim (a riff on Blake Griffin's leap over the hood of a Kia). Iman would then windmill a monster jam and come back and sit on the couch with Jeremy. Landry would hand Iman a can of Sprite as his reward for throwing down a great dunk. (Good product placement, guys. Might get you an ad campaign as well.)

At least, that's how they drew it up, Jeremy told TNT's Craig Sager, who interviewed Jeremy while he sat on the bench during the second half of the Rising Stars game. "We won't get a chance to do that [dunk]," Jeremy smiled, referring to a last-minute injury to Iman. "But it was an awesome and creative idea."

"Are you still sleeping on a couch?" Sager asked, referring to the brown sofa in teammate Landry Fields's apartment. During the height of Linsanity, Landry tweeted a photo of the most famous couch in the world—the brown velour sofa in his living room. "Let the bidding begin," he joked.

After hearing Sager's question, Jeremy laughed. "I have my own place," he said with a grin.

Jeremy could finally get off Landry's couch and into a two-bedroom rental in the swanky 38th-floor residences at the W New York Downtown Hotel because the Knicks, to no one's great surprise, stepped up and guaranteed his

Someone Had a Brain Freeze

Ben & Jerry's, the Vermont-based ice cream maker, really stepped into it when they attempted to cash in by producing a limited-edition flavor known as "Taste the Lin-Sanity."

The ingredients were vanilla frozen yogurt with honey swirls and crumbled fortune cookies. The addition of the last ingredient left a bad taste in people's mouths, as some complained about the racial overtones.

Ben & Jerry's apologized and announced that crumbled waffle cookies would replace the offending ingredient.

$762,195 salary for the rest of the year. (Actually, he only received 80 percent of that amount, or $609,756, because of the shortened season.) His paycheck squarely placed him in the 1 percenters, but in NBA terms, it was chump change and the league minimum for second-year players.

Three weeks after the NBA All-Star game, during the month of March, two things happened to derail the runaway locomotive known as Linsanity:

1. Knicks' head coach Mike D'Antoni abruptly resigned.

2. Jeremy's season ended when an MRI revealed a small, chronic meniscus tear in his left knee, which necessitated immediate surgery.

Let's take D'Antoni's situation first. When Carmelo Anthony—who knocks down nearly $20 million a year—told D'Antoni to give the Lin kid a chance back in February, the Knicks' star was injured. Jeremy got his chance, the Knicks won eight of the next nine games, and the legend of Linsanity was writ large.

Then Carmelo returned to the lineup. The Knicks promptly lost eight of the next ten games, and fingers were pointed at the gunning forward for his "selfish" play. Translation: Carmelo, once the ball got into his hands in the forecourt, preferred to work his man for a shot rather than give up the ball to a teammate. Jeremy's role as the penetrating point guard practically disappeared.

D'Antoni preached a spread-the-wealth offense, which clashed with Carmelo's isolation play. Egos were involved, and things built to a head until they reached a point where D'Antoni asked for a closed-door meeting with team officials to discuss trading Anthony. D'Antoni's request for a meeting was refused, who said, *Fine. I'll resign.*

Jeremy was understandably emotional after receiving the news. Mike D'Antoni, after all, had saved his career. And now his benefactor was gone.

Meanwhile, the show must go on. Jeremy continued to play a lot of minutes as the team won six of the next seven games—but his chronically sore knee became too tender to keep playing. (Chronic injuries, which occur from repetitive stress or overuse, are slow to develop and slower to heal.) An MRI was done, and Jeremy was told to shut it down. He needed arthroscopic knee surgery to repair a partial tear of his meniscus and would miss at least six weeks of the season, which would take him into mid-May and the opening round of the NBA playoffs.

Following his procedure, Jeremy took to his Twitter account to post a picture of himself, droopy-eyed in his hospital bed, IVs all around. "Praise God for a successful surgery … road to recovery! Lets goo," he tapped out, showing that the anesthesia hadn't entirely worn off.

As Jeremy faded off the sports pages and the Twittersphere moved on to other topics, a Linsanity backlash set in. It was probably fueled by the influential magazine *Sports Illustrated*, which had splashed Jeremy on its cover for two consecutive weeks in February. One month later, though, a *Sports Illustrated* piece by Richard Hoffer titled "Over in a New York Minute" opened with the following question: "Are we done with Jeremy Lin?"

Hoffer posited that our interest in feel-good stories like Jeremy's and Tim Tebow's spanned the half-life of a Kardashian marriage. "There seems to be a new shot clock on our celebrity culture, moving people on and off the stage with increasing impatience, as if it's the velocity of the story that matters and not the story itself, speed more satisfying than substance," wrote Hoffer.[37]

Snarky, to be sure, although there was an element of truth in Hoffer's observations. Meanwhile, the *New York Post*, on its back page, created a marble tombstone with the following inscription:

R.I.P.

LINSANITY

Briefly Beloved Broadway Smash Hit

February 4, 2012

to

March 14, 2012

Perhaps Jeremy had an inkling that his days as a New York Knick were numbered as well.

Chapter 8

BACK TO THE FUTURE

A month before Jeremy went under the knife, my wife, Nicole, underwent arthroscopic surgery on her left knee to clean up a partially torn meniscus. She experienced significant post-op pain, and I witnessed her hobbling around on crutches for several weeks. We both knew it was going to take months before she regained complete mobility. And Jeremy was supposed to come back and put his repaired knee under the crucible of professional basketball in six weeks, good as new?

I know there's a considerable physical difference between a middle-aged mom and a superbly conditioned athlete in the prime of his life, but I didn't see how Jeremy was going to be ready for the rigors of NBA basketball in six short weeks. That's why it was no surprise to me that Jeremy wasn't cleared by team doctors to play during the first round of the NBA playoffs between the Knicks and the Miami Heat. The series was a mere bump in the road for the LeBron-led Heat, who won the best-of-seven series in five games and used that victory as a springboard to claim the NBA championship a month later.

So what was next for Jeremy? His situation with the Knicks was up in the air because he was a restricted free agent, meaning the Knicks could match any contract offer he received. Because of the intricacies of the NBA's collective bargaining agreement and the salary cap, the conventional wisdom was that the Knicks would match any offer sheet. Most observers agreed that Jeremy figured to see a significant upgrade in salary—perhaps $5 million a season on a multiyear contract.

But did the Knicks want Jeremy? You have to figure the answer was yes, if for no other reason than Jeremy made Madison Square Garden a rollicking place to watch basketball again. Spike Lee, the filmmaker who always sat courtside, said Linsanity was the loudest he'd ever heard the Garden. You add in how Jeremy put butts in the seats, lifted TV ratings on the Knicks' MSG Network, sold a ton of merchandise, and gave the Knicks street cred, and you figured a deal would get done for arguably the most popular player in the NBA.

The plan all along was for Jeremy to test the market and see what other teams were willing to pay. His agent, Robert Montgomery with Montgomery Sports Group, couldn't start contacting other teams until July 1, 2012, the first day of the NBA's free agency period. While all parties were in a holding pattern, Knicks' head coach

Mike Woodson made a trip out to Los Angeles in late June to visit Carmelo Anthony and Tyson Chandler. Woodson called Jeremy and said he wanted to see him too, so Jeremy—who was back in his old bedroom at his parents' Palo Alto home for the summer—hopped on a commuter flight to LA. He met Woodson and his teammates at Mastro's Steakhouse in Beverly Hills, and it was like old times. Woodson reiterated that Jeremy was his guy at point guard, that everything would work out on the offensive side of the ball between Jeremy and Carmelo, and that the Knicks were going places. They wanted Jeremy in the mix.

Jeremy left the dinner on a high. "I walked away like, 'This is sweet.' I was thinking, *I'm excited*. Before that dinner, I had reservations. Afterward, I was like, 'Yeah, this is going to be good,'" he told writer Will Leitch of *GQ* magazine.[38]

Initially, no team tendered a contract offer right after the July 1 deadline, probably figuring that Jeremy was a lock to return to the Knicks. Then Montgomery was told by the Knicks organization, *Oh, by the way, we're also looking at other point guards*. The list included Steve Nash, Jason Kidd, and Andre Miller, who were all thirty-six years or older—creaky-old by NBA standards.

How do you interpret that shot across the bow? Montgomery worked the phones on behalf of his client, and three teams got into the mix. One of them was the Houston Rockets—the last team to waive Jeremy before the Knicks rescued him from oblivion. Rockets' general

manager Daryl Morey, along with his counterpart at the
Golden State Warriors, received a ration of fan abuse
during the height of Linsanity, prompting Morey to go to
his Twitter back in February 2012. "We should have kept
@JLin7. Did not know he was this good. Anyone who says
they knew misleading U," he tweeted.

Jeremy and his agent flew to Houston, where they were
courted by Morey, who said all the right things—how
sorry they were they cut him, that it was all a big mistake
and it never should have happened, blah, blah, blah. But
as is often in the case in these sorts of negotiations, money
speaks louder than words. Morey pushed a sizable offer
across the table—three years and $19 million.

We'll match that, said the Knicks.

This was high-stakes poker. Morey heard the call and
threw more chips into the pile—three years and $25
million, with a third-year raise to $14.9 million. (Jeremy
was prevented from earning more than $5 million and
$5,225,000 in the first two years by the collective bargain-
ing agreement's "Gilbert Arenas" provision.) In NBA nego-
tiating terms, the big payout in the third year was known
as a "poison pill" because that amount would impose a
sizable luxury tax on the Knicks for paying its players
much more money than players on other teams.

All Jeremy and his agent could do was wait and see
what the Knicks would do. A few days later, Jeremy was
surfing the Web when a headline popped out and caught
his eye: **Knicks acquire Felton in sign-and-trade with**

Blazers.[39] Felton was free agent point guard Raymond Felton of the Portland Trail Blazers. Known for being "portly," the barrel-chested Felton was coming off a poor season but had been working out like crazy and was said to have dropped twenty pounds.

Collateral Damage

When the New York Knicks decided not to re-sign Jeremy Lin, the decision sent ripples throughout Gotham, according to the satirical website Sports Pickle.

"New York Post Lays Off Its 32-Person Jeremy Lin Pun Staff," blared a boldface headline on the sportspickle.com website, which was the springboard to a hilarious story that sure sounded like it was true.

> "I'm out of a job," confirmed Jeff Sierman, who ran the Post's 32-person Jeremy Lin pun staff. "I thought the Knicks would keep Jeremy forever and that I would have as much job security as you can in this business. But, suddenly, I'm jobless and desperate for linterviews."

The faux story continued with this:

> Most of the New York media members who have lost their jobs due to Lin's departure will seek jobs in Houston, where Lin will play with the Rockets. But there will be far fewer Lin pun-based jobs there. "HousLIN has less of a tabloid LINdustry," said Sierman.[40]

The decision to trade for Felton meant only one thing to Jeremy. He was no longer a New York Knick; they were going with someone else. Since the team would not match Houston's offer sheet, it was good-bye Big Apple.

Jeremy, by all indications, wanted to stay in New York. He knew better than anyone else that something special had happened with the rise of Linsanity, but this time the ball wasn't in his hands. Someone else was directing traffic on the court, and his days of playing basketball as a New York Knick were over. It really *was* Linsanity, R.I.P.

Daryl Morey took to his Twitter account with a personal message to Jeremy and all Rockets fans: "Welcome to Houston @Jlin7! We plan to hang on this time."

A New Play Call

A few weeks after Jeremy signed his new contract with the Houston Rockets, he gave an interview to Marcus Thompson II, a beat reporter with the *San Jose Mercury News*. Thompson has followed Jeremy for a couple of years and written about him extensively dating back to rookie season with the Golden State Warriors. I know that because I read a lot of those articles while researching *Playing with Purpose* and *Linspired*. I can tell that Jeremy trusts Thompson because he says things to him he doesn't say anywhere else.

Thompson asked Jeremy if all the Linsanity craziness went to his head.

"If I'm being honest, in some ways, yes," he replied. "I fought it every day. But I think subconsciously it had its effect, everyone catering to you."

Jeremy wouldn't be human if he wasn't aware of what was happening around him on the island of Manhattan during February 2012. The number of words written about him—in the traditional media, in the blogosphere, and sent into cyberspace via Twitter and Facebook—was absolutely mind-boggling. When you add in ESPN's twenty-four-hour news cycle and all those chattering voices eager to say their piece, I could see where Jeremy would be overwhelmed.

And then came the backlash—the Linsanity tombstones, the Bronx cheers, and those who said Jeremy was overrated.

"People were saying only good things for so long that when people said negative stuff, it was like, 'Whoa, what's going on?'" Jeremy said to Thompson, who wrote this:

> After Lin signed a three-year, $25 million contract with the Houston Rockets, a lot of negative things were said. He's selfish. He's all about the money. His ego is out of control. And, to top it off, many deemed him a basketball fluke who already has maxed out his potential.
>
> But Lin is happy. He said he is thankful for his time in New York with the Knicks, the ride of a lifetime. He said he is eager about his future in Houston

and the possibilities with his new team. And he doesn't seem too concerned with repairing his image or proving himself right. He said too much is going well to be worried about the negative.

"It's not about who's right or wrong. I'm going to respond with love," Lin said. "That's why I'm in this position, to show love and become a better person. I'm trying to focus on the right things. I'm thankful for everything that's happened. The Lord has blessed me so much."[41]

If Jeremy really wanted to max out his celebrity, he could have signed a huge book deal for his autobiography. He did not. He could have said yes to any number of endorsement deals, but he only added two companies —Volvo cars and Steiner Sports (a sports memorabilia company)—to his Nike deal, which was already in place before Linsanity.

Now a whole new chapter was starting in Texas, and nothing would ever be the same as before.

A New Situation

The first thing Jeremy did when he arrived in Houston was regain his old No. 7 jersey number.

The Rockets, who were barely above .500 during the short 2011–12 season (34–32), went through a major housecleaning during the offseason. Five of their top six scorers were let go, and four of the replacements were rookies, like Donatas Motiejûnas, a Lithuanian seven-footer who came to the NBA from the Polish League. With the NBA's lowest payroll—$48 million, which is half that of the Los Angeles Lakers—the Rockets' biggest hopes were making the playoffs.

Let's just say that Jeremy wasn't dribbling into the greatest basketball situation.

But that all changed with a blockbuster deal as the 2012–13 season began—when the Rockets and Oklahoma City Thunder traded seven players and three draft picks. The big catch for the Rockets was the NBA's Sixth Man of the Year for the 2011–12 season—James Harden, a left-handed swingman with a sweet 3-point shot and an ability to score at will from the perimeter. Harden is an elite ballplayer who is likely to be among the Top Ten scorers in the NBA now that he's getting a lot more minutes with the Rockets.

Suddenly, with Harden in the lineup, the Rockets were sporting the best backcourt in the NBA—or at least one of the most exciting. Harden wears a long, Moses-length beard, a good indication that Jeremy and James are spiritually in sync as well.

"I just want to thank God for everything he has done in my life," Harden tweeted after he scored 37 points in his debut game with the Rockets. "I really am a believer. All glory to the man above."[42] Harden has been photographed wearing the same **In Jesus' Name I Play** rubber wrist-bands as Jeremy.

With Harden scoring buckets by the bushel and Jeremy running the offense, the Jeremy Lin Show sets up the big tent in Houston, at least for the foreseeable future. As with anything in life, it will be interesting to see how it all plays out.

Chapter 9

LESSONS FROM AN ASIAN-AMERICAN TRAILBLAZER

Back when Jeremy signed with the Golden State Warriors in the summer of 2010 but before the start of training camp, he was talking with a female friend who was on the Stanford tennis team. They were chatting about life when she mentioned she knew Amber Liu, an Asian-American athlete from San Diego who had a spectacular career playing tennis for Stanford. Amber won the NCAA singles championship twice and was a four-time All-American.

Amber had married the greatest — and most famous — Asian-American athlete ever: Michael Chang, who in 1989 became the youngest male to win a Grand Slam tournament when he captured the French Open at the age of seventeen. No player of Asian ancestry had ever won one of tennis's coveted major tournaments.

Michael's unprecedented victory in Paris electrified the Asian-American community and was a source of pride.

Here was one of their own standing atop the sporting world. A picture of him falling into the salmon-colored *terre battue* of Roland Garros at his moment of triumph was plastered across the front page of many newspapers around the world. Michael then proved that he wasn't a one-Slam wonder by fashioning a fourteen-year Hall of Fame career that saw him rise to No. 2 in the tennis world.

Jeremy was nine months old—not even dunking Nerf balls yet—when Michael made history in Paris. One can only imagine what Gie-Ming and Shirley were thinking, but Michael's success certainly opened a mental door that had been closed up to that point. *Anything was possible in America if you worked hard enough.*

Jeremy asked his Stanford friend if she would help him reach Michael because he wanted to ask him some questions. Jeremy's rookie season with the Golden State Warriors was beginning, and this whole professional athlete thing was new to him. Who better to know what he was going through than Michael Chang—someone who was a hero to the Asian-American community?

"I talked with Michael before the season started and asked him about being a Christian in professional sports," Jeremy told me. "I picked up some good ideas, like having a consistent devotional time and a prayer team behind you. So I formed a small team that I sent e-mails to every once in a while with prayer requests and praise reports."

The fact that Jeremy reached out to Michael Chang for advice on athletic and spiritual matters before Linsanity reveals a lot about Jeremy's character. Here was a young man willing to be mentored. "As iron sharpens iron, so one person sharpens another," Proverbs 27:17 reminds us.

After Linsanity had run its course, I called Michael to talk about Jeremy. We had the following conversation:

What do you remember about Jeremy's phone call to you before the start of his rookie season? Were you surprised that he found you? Or that he even knew that you played tennis, since there is such an age difference between the two of you? (Michael is forty years old; Jeremy is seventeen years younger.)

Michael Chang: When we spoke on the phone, I tried to be a source of encouragement for Jeremy. I don't want to go into exact detail about what we talked about, but I knew Jeremy had done very well at Harvard. He asked me what it's like to play professionally, what were some of the things he could expect in dealing with players who had been out there, what it was like dealing with coaches — stuff like that.

From a spiritual perspective, we talked about how to deal with pressures and expectations and managing our walk in Christ. Obviously, with the way the schedule is in the NBA, it's very difficult to go to church on Sunday because you're either traveling or playing. In my case, when I was playing overseas, it was even more difficult because a lot of churches don't have services in English.

Jeremy said that you talked to him about having a

consistent devotional time, a prayer team behind him. Can you talk more about that?

Michael Chang: I think having a prayer team behind you is really, really important. When I was going through difficult things in my career, knowing I had a few hundred people praying for me was huge. That kind of support goes a long way, especially when we sent out prayer requests so people knew where I was and what I was going through. For instance, if I was dealing with an injury or dealing with a difficult circumstance or had a tough match coming up, it was good to know I had my brothers and sisters in Christ on their knees praying for me.

I believe Jeremy has done that. I think he has a team that he sends an e-mail out to and shares prayer requests with. I think it's very important to do that. In addition, your daily walk — the time you yourself spend with the Lord — becomes instrumental in staying grounded, knowing what's right and wrong and being able to recognize the difference.

Discernment is important because sometimes you don't know a person's intentions until you really get to know them a little bit. The tough thing is that when you're doing well, everybody is your friend. It's not easy to distinguish sometimes between friends and those who don't have your best interests in mind.

With all this sudden fame that happened overnight, what does Jeremy need to pay attention to? After all,

the same experience of overnight success happened to you when you won the French Open at the age of seventeen.

Michael Chang: I think Jeremy right now needs to be able to manage his time well. He has to physically take care of himself, keep himself fresh, and allow himself to eat well, drink well, and get enough rest.

All of that becomes more difficult now because of the demands placed on him at this time. He's got a lot more press to manage. A lot more interviews to do. Certainly a lot more autograph signing and pictures. I'm sure he's dealing with agents and possible endorsements.

He's got a lot of things on his plate now. I think they're all good things, but he needs to be able to manage everything well, keeping a proper perspective and having his priorities straight. Certainly some adjustments will have to be made. I think one of the best ways to deal with everything is to have a good support team around him and certainly to stay close to the Lord because you can't do everything and you can't please everybody.

Talk to those of us who have never been to the Far East about how famous Jeremy is in China and Taiwan.

Michael Chang: I mean, honestly speaking, it's crazier in Asia than in the United States for Jeremy. It's different in Asia because there aren't as many famous people, as many superstars, so the media attention and paparazzi don't get dispensed so much.

Here in the United States, it's like, "Oh, there's so and so, and there's so and so." But in Asia, when you see someone famous, it's like, "WOW!"

The attention and the photographers and people following you around—let's face it, it can get intense. I know his family back in Taiwan is being bombarded by press wherever they go. It's harder to hide over there. When you go to a place like Taiwan or Hong Kong, people will watch your every move; they will follow you everywhere, and it becomes very, very difficult to step out of your hotel room.

Did you see Linsanity coming? Because nobody could have predicted this ...

Michael Chang: No, I don't think anybody did. I know that Jeremy had worked really, really hard in the off-season. Obviously he didn't really have the opportunity to go out and play for Golden State or Houston. He got a couple of minutes here and a couple of minutes there, but he never got the opportunity to start. Houston was particularly tough because they had so many great point guards.

I think his opportunity in New York was a God thing. My understanding is that Carmelo Anthony actually went to the coach during the New Jersey game and said, "Hey, I think you should play Jeremy in the second half." To hear that from your star player means something. The coach heard that and put him in, and in the second half Jeremy scored something like 24 points in that first game.

Obviously he was ready to play, and I was excited for him and really happy that he played his heart out and didn't worry about all the other things going on around him.

I'm impressed that you know his story so well. It seems you've been following Jeremy pretty closely.

Michael Chang: I have. It's been exciting. I have been able to watch some of his games on TV, and it's been nice to be able to see someone with a similar background play basketball in the NBA. He was born and raised in the United States like me, he's an Asian-American, and he came from humble beginnings. On top of that, he's a brother in Christ.

I would love to see him do well. For me that would be very exciting because I can't say there are a whole lot of people I can put in that category. There have been a few young women like Michelle Kwan, Kristi Yamaguchi, and Michelle Wie, but as far as the men's side goes, I can't say there have been a lot of top Asian-American athletes. For the most part, I have a fair amount of things in common with Jeremy.

Did you play much basketball when you were a kid, or were you too short?

Michael Chang: I played a lot of basketball. There is one misnomer that maybe people don't understand: Asians love to play basketball. We've had our Christian sports leagues in Seattle and Orange County [organized by the Chang Family Foundation] and pickup games at church, and man, it's packed with Asian-American players.

We've never had anybody break through in the NBA, and up until now, the most famous Asian player has been Yao Ming, but I think it's a little bit easier to relate to Jeremy since he's six foot three. Obviously, that is still pretty tall for someone of Asian descent, but not like Yao Ming at seven foot six. But Asians love to play basketball, and I count myself among that group.

How much basketball did you play growing up in Southern California?

Michael Chang: Yeah, I played quite a bit when it was basketball season. I wouldn't drive to the basket like Jeremy does because I didn't want to get elbowed or get hurt before a tournament. I'd stay outside and try to play good defense and shoot from the outside.

Have you ever seen Jeremy play in person? If not, will you go see him play when he's in Los Angeles playing against the Lakers or the Clippers?

Michael Chang: I would love to have the opportunity to go see him play in person. I have never met Jeremy, but I have met his mom and his brother. They came out to talk with Carl and me when I had a speaking engagement in the Bay Area. [Carl is Michael's older brother, a fine tennis player, who was Michael's coach during his career.] This was just after he had signed with Golden State. Mrs. Lin wanted some of our thoughts on Jeremy's career, and I got a chance to talk with her. But no, I've never met Jeremy.

Have you been sending him any texts?

Michael Chang: Yes, I have been sending him some encouragement through texts.

Have your parents spoken with his parents? Since they are all from Taiwan, I would imagine they have a lot in common.

Michael Chang: They never actually met, but I think that my dad has been on some phone calls with his mom when she called Carl. From a sports perspective, we have a fair amount of experience dealing with agents and sponsors, which we were happy to share.

For us to have the opportunity to encourage the younger generation, whether it is Jeremy or another tennis player or young junior coming up—we try to take advantage of that. I feel that the Lord has given us a fair amount of knowledge, and there is no reason to hold any of that back. We want to just encourage this next generation to get the most out of the talent that God has given each one of them.

I envision that with Jeremy's success, a number of temptations will come his way. What can he expect? How can he best deal with this?

Michael Chang: I think it's important for him to stay grounded in the Word, to spend a lot of good quality time with the Lord.

Unfortunately, the way I understand it, things can get a little bit crazy in the NBA. We have obviously heard a lot of different stories about players in the past and some of the challenges they had to deal with.

When I was on the pro tour, A. C. Green was playing for the Lakers. He often talked about how he was willing to wait for marriage before having sex and how difficult it was to keep that commitment when you're a Christian who is playing in the NBA. Hopefully, players will respect that Jeremy has certain values and morals that he is not willing to compromise. That is really, really important, but I also think it's great he is so outspoken about his faith. When someone is that outspoken about his faith, it sets a certain precedence. people are a little less likely to ask you to do something or to be a part of something, knowing that your faith takes first precedence in your life.

I think Jeremy has a good head on his shoulders. You can see it in the way he gives his interviews. He is very humble and gives a lot of credit to the Knicks' staff and is very complimentary toward his fellow players.

Hopefully, he'll be a great influence on them, not only on the basketball court but off it as well.

Looking to China

I've never been west of Hawaii, and the vast majority of Americans haven't been past the International Date Line either, so Michael Chang is right: we have no idea what a big deal Jeremy is in Asia. For the past two summers, Jeremy has made several trips to China and Taiwan after the NBA season was over.

Jeremy's Asian heritage has triggered a fan frenzy throughout Asia, but in China, the reaction has been particularly intense. He's a hot topic on television sports talk shows, and his Chinese name, Lin Shuhao—the surname is said first in the Chinese cultural sphere—ranks among the most searched items on Baidu, China's largest search engine.

Jeremy's ascendency is great timing for Chinese basketball and for the NBA, whose largest overseas market is China. A void was created when Yao Ming, the seven-foot-six center, retired in the summer of 2011 following two seasons of nagging foot and ankle problems that were severely limiting his play.

The heir apparent to the Ming dynasty is now Jeremy, and you can bet your last *yuan* that NBA league officials are at work right now to position Jeremy as the new face of the NBA's global empire. He speaks Mandarin but is not fluent, having learned the tonal language from his parents while growing up. They spoke to him in Mandarin, but he replied in English—as kids often do when they speak nothing but English outside the front door.

"I'm a lot better listening to it than I am speaking it," Jeremy said. "My Mandarin could definitely use some work."[43] He took a few classes at Harvard University to improve his reading and writing skills.

After Jeremy signed his rookie contract with Golden

Yao Ming: The Jeremy Connection

When American basketball fans think of Asians who play the game, their first thought is Yao Ming, the skyscraper-tall center for the Houston Rockets who retired in 2011.

Yao wasn't the tallest player ever to play in the NBA—seven-foot-seven centers Manute Bol and Gheorghe Muresan share that distinction—but he was almost half a foot taller than Pau Gasol, Dirk Nowitzki, and Shaquille O'Neal, as well as Kareem Abdul-Jabbar and Wilt Chamberlain, for that matter. Throughout his eight-year injury-plagued career, Yao was the face of basketball in Asia.

His background is a fascinating story. There are indications that Chinese athletic officials strongly "encouraged" the marriage of two of their basketball stars—a six-foot-nine man, Yao Zhiyuan, and a six-foot-three woman, Fang Fengdi—with the hope that they would successfully produce a basketball center the likes of which the world had never seen.

Fang Fengdi, the captain of China's women's basketball team,

State in the summer of 2010, he received a phone call from Yao Ming, who invited Jeremy to join the Yao Foundation in Taiwan for a goodwill trip that included helping out at children's basketball camps and playing in a charity basketball game in Taipei. Jeremy, his parents, and his two brothers jumped at the chance to be involved.

In Taipei, Jeremy scored 17 points for "Team Love,"

readily agreed to the grand experiment proposed by Chinese sports officials. The pairing of two very tall people produced only one child, however, and one can surmise Mama Fang must have had second thoughts about going through childbirth a second time after the excruciatingly difficult delivery of an eleven-pound baby boy.

As far as the Chinese basketball federation was concerned, Yao Ming's birth was just the beginning. When Yao was eight years old, government officials placed him in a sports school, where he would practice five afternoons a week and on Saturdays. Yao hated being forced to play basketball, but he resigned himself to practice out of respect for his parents.

Although he loathed the game for a long time and wasn't a very good player until his late teens, Yao Ming eventually discovered his game and became an international star. But his brittle body couldn't withstand the pounding underneath the basket, which is why we'll never get a chance to see an NBA matchup featuring Yao Ming and Jeremy Lin.

which was comprised of NBA players that included Brandon Jennings of the Milwaukee Bucks, Amir Johnson of the Toronto Raptors, and Hasheem Thabeet of the Memphis Grizzlies. Jeremy's paternal grandmother, Lin Chu A-muen—who still lives in Taiwan—cheered on her grandson. Their competition was Team Heart, made up of players from the Shanghai Sharks and All-Stars from the local Super Basketball League.

The Shanghai Sharks were owned by none other than Yao Ming. Yao and Jeremy bonded during the goodwill trip and have stayed in touch since then. In fact, during the NBA lockout prior to Linsanity, Yao attempted to sign Jeremy to play for the Shanghai Sharks, a team Yao once played for, but Jeremy turned down his new friend because leaving American soil to play in China probably would have snuffed out his dream of making his mark in the NBA.

Jeremy also received strong interest from Euroleague powerhouse Maccabi Tel Aviv in Israel—it would have been fascinating for Jeremy to play a season in the Holy Land—and from Teramo Basket, a club in the Italian League.

Many Americans don't realize that ever since James Naismith invented basketball 120 years ago, this team sport has evolved into a game played worldwide, in more than 200 countries, by men and women, young and old, able-bodied and physically challenged.

The "Dream Team" that assembled during the 1992

Barcelona Olympics took the world by storm, setting the stage for an explosion of interest in basketball beyond our nation's borders. Players like Michael Jordan of the Chicago Bulls, Larry Bird of the Boston Celtics, Charles Barkley of the Philadelphia 76ers, Patrick Ewing of the New York Knicks, and Magic Johnson of the Los Angeles Lakers were treated like basketball royalty. "It was like Elvis and the Beatles put together," remarked Chuck Daly, the Team USA coach.

It's no coincidence that the globalization of the NBA picked up like a fast break after the Dream Team exited Barcelona with gold medals draped over their U.S. Olympic team outfits. NBA teams toured Europe and played exhibition games against top national teams, as well as against "friendlies" in Asia and South America.

Thanks to these trailblazing efforts, kids in South America, in Europe, in Africa, in Asia — especially China and Taiwan — became passionate about basketball. They play and practice the game and proudly wear NBA jerseys featuring their favorite players. The NBA estimates that 300 million people in China play basketball.

Jeremy has earned a boatload of frequent flier miles traveling to the Far East the last couple of years. He visited China for the first time in May 2011, playing in a friendly match at a middle school in Pinghu and visiting his family's ancestral home in northern China's Zhejiang province. Camera crews and photographers followed him everywhere, and he became immensely popular because of the prominent media coverage. Some authorities in mainland China tried to claim him as one of their own since his maternal grandmother had grown up in China, but Jeremy and his family have identified themselves as Taiwanese, which creates an interesting dynamic since

Foreign Players in the NBA

When the "Dream Team" captured the gold medal at the 1992 Barcelona Olympics, there were only twenty foreign-born players in the NBA at the start of the 1992–93 season—just 6 percent of the total number of players in the league.

That number has changed quickly in the last two decades as players like Yao Ming of China, Dirk Nowitzki of Germany, Steve Nash of Canada, Andrew Bogut of Australia, Tony Parker of France, Omri Casspi of Israel, and Pau Gasol of Spain brought their sterling A games to the NBA. General managers have undertaken full-blown international scouting efforts, a tacit acknowledgment that the big gap between the NBA game and the rest of the world has virtually disappeared.

Here's where we are today: at the start the 2012–13 season, there were eighty-four international players from thirty-seven countries, or a bit more than 20 percent of the total number of players. Some say we're seeing more foreign-born participants in the NBA because they are fundamentals-driven players known for their pinpoint passes, surefire shooting, and team-first attitudes.

mainland China views the island of Taiwan as a renegade province.

While Jeremy was in China, the state news media was careful not to talk too much about Taiwan or mention his faith—a taboo topic since China is an atheist state. Internet searches related to Jeremy's faith have been blocked in China. It will be interesting to see how this plays out in the future.

Jeremy made a second visit to China a few months later, in September 2011, during the lockout. He played in a few games for the Dongguan Leopards, a team in the Chinese Basketball Association that was competing in the ABA Club Championship in Guangzhou, China. Jeremy was named Most Valuable Player, and once again, he was big news in the Chinese media.

Of course, *everything* changed after Linsanity. Traveling to Taiwan and China during the summer of 2012 amped up everything times ten in terms of media attention and fan interest. In Taiwan, Jeremy participated in a four-day summer camp, where he coached more than a hundred young basketballers, played shoot-and-giggle exhibitions for charity, and participated in a televised evangelical gathering. He also visited his Taiwanese relatives, including his grandmother, and family members said his Mandarin had improved since his last visit a year earlier.

As you can imagine, Jeremy dominated the news cycle while he was in Taiwan. Cameras followed him everywhere, and as Michael Chang predicted, it was difficult to leave his hotel room without security clearing a path for him. Jeremy and his entourage (including brother Josh and trainer Josh Fan) decided to have a little fun with the situation. They enlisted Pete Radovich, creative director of CBS Sports, to put together a short film of Jeremy planning his "escape" from the paparazzi in Taiwan with a late-night breakout from their hotel to play hoops with the locals.

I've watched the 6 minute 11 second video, titled "A Late Night Escape in Taipei."[44] The film opens with Jeremy setting off Beatlemania-like screams and hundreds of camera flashes upon his arrival out of customs at Taipei Songshan Airport. The scene shifts to Jeremy, leaning against a plate-glass window of a fancy downtown hotel. "Did you see how many cameras there are outside? How are we going to get out of here?" he asks his brother.

They hatch a plan to sneak out of the hotel with Jeremy wearing a giant Hello Kitty head—like anyone would be fooled. (A lot of the moments in the film were obviously staged, which is part of the fun.) They enlist David Lee of the Golden State Warriors to join them, and miraculously, they walk past dozens of camera crews who fail to notice three guys and a dude matching the size of Jeremy Lin wearing a ridiculous foam head.

You can imagine the outcome. They drive to the Xinsheng courts (under some bridge or freeway overpass) and begin hooping it up with the locals, who all know who Jeremy is. Dozens of cell phones are raised to record the moment, and they let the games begin. Jeremy freelances amazing move after amazing move, drawing oohs and aahs.

"That was pure basketball," Jeremy says as the car makes its way back to the hotel. "That was fun." A local reporter on the late news breathlessly describes how Jeremy's foray "turned a late night into frenzy."

Before he departed Taiwan, reporters tried to trap him by asking Jeremy whether he viewed himself as Chinese or Taiwanese, but he showed he could make some adept moves off the court by successfully evading this touchy question, saying, "There's a lot of history behind who I am."

Then the Jeremy Lin Show moved on to China, where Jeremy visited an elementary school for children of migrant workers in a Beijing suburb, appeared on a TV show called *China's Got Talent*, and conducted a four-day basketball camp in Dongguan, where he had played a few games for the Leopards during the NBA lockout. His final stop was in Hong Kong, where Jeremy held up a sign listing his activities on a typical day:

- Basketball Training: 5 hours

- Bible Reading: 1/2 hour

- Family Time & Relaxing: 3 hours

Once again, in Hong Kong, Jeremy was asked about his nationality—whether he considered himself Chinese, Taiwanese, or American.

His reply was pure Jeremy: "My identity is in Christ."[45]

Chapter 10

LINSANITY AND TEBOWMANIA

Just as I don't think Jeremy Lin will disappear, I don't believe we've heard the last about Tim Tebow, who set off another pop culture phenomenon—Tebowmania —when he came off the bench and rescued the Denver Broncos from oblivion during the 2011 season, just weeks before Linsanity came out of nowhere.

What is amazing to me about Linsanity and Tebowmania is that neither Jeremy nor Tim hid the fact that they were followers of Christ, but the media—which are largely secular—were still drawn to them. It's as though they sensed the fragrance of Christ permeating from their pores.

Columnists, reporters, and pundits took measure of the two and came to the conclusions that Jeremy and Tim genuinely believed in the faith that defines them and that they approached life in a spirit of humbleness. They noticed how the two refused to "impose" their faith through being preachy or employing silly clichés ("The Man Upstairs was looking out for us today"). Instead, both athletes spoke thoughtfully and reflectively, whether Christ was overtly part of the conversation or not.

When Tim was quarterbacking the Broncos to all those victories, he was ripped by television host and political commentator Bill Maher, who profanely and rudely made fun of him—via Twitter—after the Bronco quarterback tossed three interceptions in a loss to the Buffalo Bills. Sally Jenkins of the *Washington Post* rushed to Tim's defense. "Anyone who listens to Tebow knows he doesn't do Jesus talk; he's mostly show-and-tell," she wrote. "His idea of proselytizing is to tweet an abbreviated Bible citation. Mark 6:36. He leaves it up to you whether to look it up. When he takes a knee, it's perfectly obvious that it's an expression of humility. He's crediting his perceived source, telling himself, *Don't forget where you came from.* On the whole, it's more restrained than most end-zone shimmies."[46]

There are more similarities than you think between the two young athletes, even though they play different sports and come from different ethnic backgrounds. They are both under the age of twenty-six and close in age—Tim is older by one year, having been born on August 14, 1987. Each came off the bench when their teams' seasons were going down in flames and fans' patience was stretched to the breaking point. Each made their career relevant by immediately winning—Tim took the Broncos on a six-game winning streak in 2011, and Linsanity ignited seven straight wins for the Knicks in February 2012.

On the spiritual side of the ledger, Jeremy and Tim were raised by parents who were Christians before they were born, and that is notable. This means they were raised in the "admonition of the Lord" from birth and were raised under the guidance of Proverbs 22:6, which reminds parents to "start children off on the way they should go, and even when they are old they will not turn from it."

Jeremy said his parents brought him up in a Christian home and taught him what it means to be a believer. "But the thing I appreciate most about them is they don't judge my basketball performance on how I do individually in terms of statistics," he said in a March 2010 interview with studentsoul.org when he was at Harvard. "They make sure I have the right attitude, that I don't yell at my teammates or the refs and that I'm always under control. They make sure I have a godly attitude and when I don't, they call me out on it and make me accountable."[47]

Tim, when interviewed by *NFL Today* host James Brown, said he was taught a similar perspective by his parents. "What my mom and dad preached to me when I was a little kid: Just because you have athletic ability and may be able to play a sport doesn't make you any more special than anybody else. Doesn't mean God loves you more than anybody else. We play a sport. It's a game. At the end of the day, that's all it is, it's a game. It doesn't make you any better or any worse than anybody else. So by winning a game, you're no better. By losing a game, you're no worse. I think by keeping that mentality, it really keeps things in perspective for me to treat everybody the same."[48]

Another parallel is that Jeremy and Tim were raised in homes where their parents weren't afraid to discipline their children when they fell out of line or showed willful disobedience. The parents understood the teaching of Proverbs 12:1, which reads, "Whoever loves discipline loves knowledge, but whoever hates correction is stupid." Michael Chang said that when he had disobeyed his parents as a very young boy, his father would direct him to kneel on the floor and stretch his arms in front of him. "You will keep your arms out as long as I want," said Michael's father. The tennis star said it always seemed like a long time before this form of punishment—known as a *fa-gua* in the Chinese culture—was declared over.

Learning discipline helped both Jeremy and Tim set goals and attain them, the resilience of getting back on their feet when life knocked them down, and the value of never giving up.

Jeremy and Tim have shown discipline in the way they answer questions from the media. They are careful not to give their opponents anything that can be used against them or their team—known as "blackboard material" that can get posted up in the opposing locker room. If you listen closely, any time they are asked about what they did to win the game or orchestrate a comeback, they quickly deflect the attention away from themselves. They turn that line of inquiry into an opportunity to give props to their teammates, coaching staff, or front office.

In fact, both have shown wisdom beyond their years in the way they handle the media. After leading the Knicks to their seventh straight win during Linsanity, Jeremy reflected thoughtfully on this phase of his life. "I want to be able to sit back when I'm done with my career and say that I gave everything I could and that I did it for God's glory," he told Dan Duggan of the *Boston Herald*. "When I say do it for God's glory, there are a lot of things I want to do off the court in terms of the platform of an NBA player to be able to impact the world. I'm thankful for the platform, but I don't want people to lose sight of the team, because without the team, I'm nothing."[49]

See what I'm talking about? Jeremy is right about the platform part too, because playing a major sport on a national stage lends itself to all sorts of opportunities.

Take, for instance, what Tim has done with his platform. For the last two seasons at Denver and in New York with the Jets, Tim has invited young people with serious medical challenges to meet him on the sidelines before *and* after each game, home and away. It touches your heart big-time to see these teenagers who have life-threatening diseases or who are physically disfigured because of their illnesses light up when Tim Tebow—*Tim Tebow!*—enters their lives to tell them that God loves them and that Tim will be praying for them.

Those who've gotten a chance to meet Tim are part of the Tebow Foundation's "Wish 15" program—15 is Tim's jersey number—which grants wishes to kids and young people facing serious medical problems. Tim's foundation gives him a platform to bring faith, hope, and love to those who need it and has resulted in the construction of a hospital in the Philippines—the country where Tim was born to missionary parents.

Jeremy now has his own foundation, naturally named the Jeremy Lin Foundation, which is dedicated to reaching out to underprivileged individuals and communities to provide financial, educational, and spiritual assistance. During his last off-season, Jeremy found time to visit elementary schools in the San Francisco Bay Area and bring items for the schools' food drives.

Getting Acquainted

During Linsanity, it didn't take long for the media to track down the man behind Tebowmania and see what he thought of the basketball player from New York. Reporters caught up with Tim on the green carpet at the Cartoon Network's Hall of Game Awards. (Don't laugh about the green carpet treatment; Shaquille O'Neal, soccer star David Beckham, and a bevy of pro athletes from different sports were in Santa Monica, California, for the star-studded event.)

"I really like him," Tim said. "I respect him a whole lot.

I've had the pleasure to really get to know him over the last few weeks. What a great guy he is. I just wish him the best of luck. How he handles himself and how he carries himself, I think he's a great role model. And I'm proud of him."

When asked what advice he could share about how Jeremy should handle the sudden burst of popularity, Tim replied, "I think he's handling himself great, and I think he can take care of himself. I'd just say keep being true to him, keep working hard, and don't listen to everybody else."[50]

They finally got to meet at the ESPY Awards in Los Angeles in July 2012 while collecting some hardware: Jeremy receiving a trophy for "Best Breakthrough Athlete," and Tim winning for "Best Moment." What was really cool about Jeremy's ESPY was that his award presenters were actress Jessica Biel and ... Tim Tebow. After listing the nominees—soccer star Alex Morgan (a female), Baylor quarterback Robert Griffin III, Kentucky hoopster Anthony Davis, and New England Patriots tight end Rob Gronkowski—Tim said the fans have spoken and announced the winner: Jeremy Lin! Afterward, Tim and Jeremy posed in comical photos with Jessica Biel—Jeremy wearing a king's crown and gigantic shades and Tim sporting a fake moustache and black-rimmed glasses—which Jeremy posted on his Twitter account.

Let's hope they get a chance to hang out longer than a backstage grip-and-grin. I'd love to see Tim show Jeremy his work at the orphanages in the Philippines (which would draw worldwide media attention), or watch Jeremy introduce Tim to China and Taiwan, where hundreds of millions of Chinese would be exposed in a subtle way to what is really important in their lives.

An E-Mail I'd Like to Write Someday

To: bigshotproducer@hollywoodstudio.com

From: mike@mikeyorkey.com

Subject: Jeremy Lin pitch

Hollywood has a long tradition of producing feel-good sports movies about athletes who overcome rejection, pilot the unexpected come-from-behind victory, or triumph by making the team, winning the championship, or going the distance against all odds. I'm thinking of films like *Rudy*, *Invincible*, *The Blind Side*, and *Rocky I*, *II*, *III*, *IV*, and *V*. Sure, they're formulaic, but overcoming hardship, adversity, and life's bad breaks is something we've all had to deal with.

Can we do lunch next week? I've got an idea to pitch your way.

* * *

Maybe my idea isn't so far-fetched. Steve Tisch, the co-owner of the New York Giants and producer of the film *Forrest Gump*, was asked if Jeremy Lin's story could translate to film.

"There are possibilities," Tisch replied. "Can Will Smith or Tom Cruise play him?"[51]

Chapter 11

A PRAYER REQUEST FOR JEREMY

When Jeremy was playing for the New York Knicks at home, there was a mini–church service for the players led by Rev. John Love, who drove nearly two hundred miles from Baltimore to New York to minister to the players. Pastor Love, who's been the youth pastor at the Greater Grace World Outreach since 1983, has served faithfully as the Knicks' chaplain for twenty-five years — and rolled off approximately 410,000 miles by my calculation.

Pastor Love keeps a low profile, which can be said for the entire NBA chaplaincy force. Many basketball fans are unaware that a chapel service is held one hour before every NBA game — regular season and playoffs. Players from both teams are welcome to attend.

This open invitation makes pro basketball different from other major sports, where players from opposing teams attend separate chapel services. National Football League players can take part in a chapel service — just for their team—on the night before their games. (All NFL teams stay in a team hotel the night before a game, whether they are at home or away.) Major League Baseball chapels are held in each team's locker rooms on Sunday mornings. Ditto for National Hockey League players.

It's different in the National Basketball Association. One hour before tip-off, players from each team are invited to an empty room located near the home and visitor locker rooms. It could be an extra locker room or even the dressing room of the team mascot. Attendance is voluntary. The home team chaplain greets the players, and maybe a song is sung a cappella.

The chaplain then speaks for ten to fifteen minutes, sharing Scripture and teaching from the Bible. The topics range from overcoming life's challenges to a reprise of the gospel message, but the basic goal is to equip the players to live lives that glorify God and to encourage them to remain strong in the face of temptation.

At the end, players sometimes share a prayer request, or they may have a question about the chaplain's message. Discussions must move quickly. Whatever direction the chaplain takes, the mini-service must end promptly at the fifteen-to-twenty-minute mark since the players are expected to be on the court shortly to warm up for the game.

After the players get loose and do some shooting around, they approach the midcourt circle for the opening tip-off. Slapped hands and fist bumps are exchanged.

Once the referee tosses the ball in the air, players from both teams—some who were seated in the same room hearing about God's love less than an hour earlier—try to soundly beat the other team, which is one of the beauties of competition.

The players from both sides, by and large, don't have any issues with meeting together before game time. They understand that being opponents doesn't matter at chapel time, because that is a time reserved for God.

"As much as these guys are competitors, they realize there are only four hundred professional basketball players in the NBA," said Jeff Ryan, chaplain for the Orlando Magic. "Playing is a privilege, not a birthright. They worked hard to get into that room. They know they are paid to perform, and they are going to play hard."

When I interviewed Jeremy, we had this exchange about the NBA chapels:

Players from both teams go to the chapel services an hour before the game. Was that something you regularly did or tried to do?

Jeremy: Yes. There were a few of us who went before every game. That was great.

It intrigues me that basketball is the only major sport in which players from both teams get together in a chapel service and then forty-five minutes later try to beat each other's brains out.

Jeremy: Yes, actually I was pretty surprised, but it's really cool to see believers from other teams. I enjoyed that a lot.

Were there more believers on other teams than you thought, or maybe fewer than you thought there would be?

Jeremy: More, definitely more. I think in the beginning you know, what I heard about the NBA, like the caution, people, like, warning me about this or that, but actually a lot of NBA players came [to the chapels]. I think NBA players as a whole get lumped into one big category, one big stereotype. I think my first year in the league I broke a lot of those stereotypes.

I realized there are a lot of Christians in the NBA. I mean it depends. A lot of people call themselves Christians—but there were a lot more people who went to chapel than I thought there would be.

Would it be generally two or three players to a team, or four or five players to a team?

Jeremy: I would probably say two to a team. Sometimes like the [Oklahoma City] Thunder, it would be ten players.

A lot of Christians on the Thunder, huh?

Jeremy: Yes, at least a lot of guys who attend chapel. I am not sure about their individual lives, but there are a lot.

On Friday, January 27, 2012, one week before the rocket launch of Linsanity, Jeremy walked down the hallway from his dressing room in Miami's American Airlines Arena to participate in the pregame chapel. The Knicks' opponent that night was the LeBron James–led Heat. Just a handful of players from both teams had joined him, including Udonis Haslem, a Miami Heat forward and a regular at the twenty-minute assemblies.

After the chaplain shared his devotional, he gently asked if anyone had a prayer request.

Jeremy raised his hand.

"That I not get cut again," he responded.[52]

Yes, his NBA playing career was that tenuous. Jeremy wasn't playing much, and his opportunity to shine against the New Jersey Nets was still in his future.

Jeremy confirmed this story in a press conference on the eve of the 2012 All-Star game in Orlando. "Yeah, I went to chapel with [Knicks teammates] Jerome Jordan and Landry Fields, and the chaplain asked us to share a prayer request. I knew February 10 was right around the corner, so that was what was on my heart, just that I would be able to continue to stay on the roster and be with the team the rest of the year."[53]

Looks like God answered that prayer in a mighty way —and the NBA should be glad too. Jeremy was *the* story of the 2011–12 season, and he played a huge role in getting people talking about professional basketball. If you think back to the darkest days of the lockout, when the NBA season should have been underway, the collective reaction among the American public was this: *Who cares about the NBA? No one pays attention until the playoffs start.*

And then Jeremy came along and made us care about professional basketball again. No matter what our team allegiance was, we were excited by Linsanity. We wanted him to succeed because we understood how difficult the demands are to play professional basketball. We wanted him to succeed because we could see the unselfish way he plays the game—straight up, with no pretense. We saw it in the way he responded with grace and humility to microphones thrust in his face. He came from a disarming place where there was no agenda.

The Linsanity story was one for the ages, a feel-good narrative that resonated with basketball fans and even those who don't pay much attention to the sport. What Jeremy accomplished in a short period of time burrows deeper than the fact that he was the first Asian-American with a Chinese/Taiwanese heritage in the NBA. It was really unfathomable that an undrafted prospect—who had logged so few minutes in the NBA—could come roaring off the bench and turn around a storied franchise in a media mecca like New York City.

Stories like Jeremy's aren't supposed to happen, but when they do, we're on our feet cheering the underdog who was told that he wasn't good enough.

Practicing the Golden Rule

We've all seen athletes—our sporting heroes—disappoint us, but I don't think fame and any success on the basketball court will spoil Jeremy. I think God was preparing him for where he's at today. He never shied away from ambition, never backed down from confrontation, and never ran away from accountability. He put himself and his game out there, and if you beat him, you were the better man that day. But if he beat you, he shook your hand and didn't gloat. That's the Golden Rule in action: *Treat others as you would want to be treated.*

He learned this teaching at a young age from his parents and from Stephen Chen, his pastor at the Chinese Church in Christ. Even before Linsanity, things had gotten a little out of hand. So many "church tourists" dropped by after his rookie season with Golden State and during the NBA lockout that Jeremy was hounded by autograph seekers and those hoping to have their picture taken with him. Things got to the point where Pastor Chen had to issue a statement from the pulpit informing everyone that Jeremy would not sign autographs or have pictures taken with him—and so "please do not bother him."

Like everyone else, Pastor Chen didn't foresee Linsanity. "I don't know if anybody could have seen it coming —Jeremy becoming essentially a global icon overnight," he said.

The New York media tracked down the Mountain View

pastor rather quickly. They wanted to know what role Jeremy's faith plays in his basketball and how his faith has helped him through an underdog type of career. Stephen felt this line of questioning came across as though the reporter was searching for some type of "prosperity gospel" angle—that if you pray hard enough and believe hard enough, then God will bless you and show favor toward you.

Pastor Chen patiently explained that things don't quite work that way. He pointed out that Jeremy's goal was obedience and true worship, as taught by Christ. He said that Jeremy acknowledged that everything happened by God's grace and for a reason, and that his success wasn't something he earned solely on his own ability and willpower.

Another line of questioning from the media focused on how Jeremy will find the strength to say no to the temptations that fame, wealth, and power will certainly thrust upon him. Pastor Chen replied that there are temptations for all Christians but that Jeremy was facing specific ones because of his success.

"Scripture talks about the devil lying in wait like a lion waiting to devour," he said. "All Christians would be foolish to underestimate the devil. That's why our church is in prayer for him. We pray that he will work heartily as for the Lord, and that he will continue to trust in God, to preach the gospel, and to look to Christ in all situations."

Jeremy and Stephen continue to talk regularly on the phone to this day, as well as text and e-mail each other.

Stephen reminds him to keep his eyes on Jesus and to watch out for any traps or temptations.

Then we had this exchange in our interview:

You realize, Stephen, that you have a very important role to play here. God has you in a very special place right now, ministering to Jeremy. I imagine that's a little heavy on your heart.

Pastor Chen: Yes, it is. It's hard because he's a member of our church, yet he's thousands of miles away. It's hard to minister to someone who is that far away. As much as he tries to go to church and wants to go to church, it's just not really possible because his schedule is very rough this year. It's hard to really build a community. We're kind of his anchor, I guess.

The Chinese Church in Christ continued to be that anchor when Jeremy flew home to Palo Alto after the Knicks lost to the Miami Heat in the opening round of the NBA playoffs. Life wouldn't the same—everyone knew that—but it was still a rude awakening when he and some buddies decided to play a little pick-up basketball at a nearby school, something he'd done since he was a little boy.

A few neighbors noticed and came by to watch, which prompted more people to stop what they were doing to come over to the playground. Commotion begat commotion, as cell phones were lifted to take pictures. After two games, Jeremy and his old friends packed it in and walked back home, trailed by young and old.

Things didn't go any better at the Chinese Church in Christ. An inordinate number of "visitors" came to the Sunday morning services hoping to see Jeremy, have a word with him, perhaps get an autograph or have a picture taken. "It wasn't exactly what I hoped for," Pastor Chen said. "We even asked one of our congregation members —a police officer—to escort Jeremy to his car because people were running him down, even following him to the parking lot. He loves the fans and is appreciative of them, but there are certain times when he would prefer not to worry about that, especially those times when he wants to worship the Lord with his friends and family."

A Final Thought

So what has Jeremy Lin wrought? What will the future bring?

No one knows how things will turn out, but that's the beauty of sport and the uncertainty of life. You never know what will happen, but we can live with the assurance that God is faithful to his own.

Now that Linsanity is over and Jeremy's playing for the Houston Rockets, perhaps he will stay under the radar for a while. He can work on his game without the bright lights of Broadway shining on him. He needs this breather more than we know.

Sooner or later, though, we'll hear from Jeremy again. Maybe we'll even see Linsanity 2.0. Whatever the future holds, the Jeremy Lin story will continue to fascinate hundreds of millions around the world. People genuinely like him, and well they should. They understand that stories like this one happen rarely. They recognize that Jeremy is an uncommon young man with uncommon leadership skills and extraordinary athletic gifts.

It all happened so fast, arriving at the busy intersection where sport, religion, fame, and pop culture meet. Jeremy handled it well, holding the Lord's hand and looking both ways before crossing the street.

Pray that as he continues his walk, his grip will remain strong.

ABOUT THE AUTHOR

Mike Yorkey, the author or coauthor of more than seventy books, has written about sports all his life for a variety of national sports publications and book publishers. He has collaborated with Cleveland Browns quarterback Colt McCoy and his father, Brad, in *Growing Up Colt*; San Francisco Giants pitcher Dave Dravecky (*Called Up* and *Play Ball*), tennis stars Michael Chang (*Holding Serve*) and Betsy McCormack (*In His Court*), and San Diego Chargers placekicker Rolf Benirschke (*Alive & Kicking*).

Mike's most recent sports book is *Believe: The Eric LeGrand Story*, the story of Rutgers football player Eric LeGrand, who was paralyzed from the neck down on a kickoff play in 2010. He has also authored *Playing with Purpose: Inside the Lives and Faith of the Major League's Top Players* (with Jesse Florea and Joshua Cooley) and *Playing with Purpose: Inside the Lives and Faith of Top NBA Stars*.

Yorkey, who graduated from the University of Oregon's School of Journalism, is a former editor of *Focus on the Family* magazine who has also written for sports magazines such as *Skiing*, *Tennis*, and *Breakaway*. He is also a novelist, and his latest fiction effort is *Chasing Mona Lisa*, a World War II thriller he coauthored with Tricia Goyer.

Mike and his wife, Nicole, are the parents of two adult children, Andrea and Patrick. Mike and Nicole make their home in Encinitas, California, and his website is www .mikeyorkey.com.

NOTES

1. Sean Gregory, "Harvard's Hoops Star Is Asian. Why's That a Problem?" *Time*, December 31, 2009, www.time.com/time/magazine/article/0,9171,1953708,00.html (accessed March 1, 2012).

2. Tim Keown, "Jeremy Lin's HS Coach Is Surprised, Too," espn.com, February 14, 2012, http://espn.go.com/espn/commentary/story/_/id/7574452/jeremy-lin-high-school-coach-surprised-too (accessed March 1, 2012).

3. Chuck Culpepper, "An All-Around Talent, Obscured by His Pedigree," *New York Times*, September 14, 2010, www.nytimes.com/2010/09/15/sports/basketball/15nba.html (accessed March 1, 2012).

4. Myrna Blyth, "Jeremy Lin Has a Tiger Mom," thirdage.com, February 17, 2012, www.thirdage.com/celebrities/jeremy-lins-tiger-mother (accessed March 1, 2012).

5. Chris Dortch, "Harvard Was Perfect Place for Lin to Hone Guard Skills," nba.com, February 17, 2012, www.nba.com/2012/news/features/chris_dortch/02/17/lin-college-break/ (accessed March 1, 2012).

6. See Gordon Govier, "NBA Rising Star Jeremy Lin Not Too Busy to Pray," *Charisma News*, February 15, 2012, http://charismanews.com/culture/32833-nba-rising-star-jeremy-lin-not-too-busy-to-pray (accessed March 1, 2012).

7. "Jeremy Lin: Taking Harvard Basketball to New Levels," StudentSoul.org, March 12, 2010, www.intervarsity.org/studentsoul/item/jeremy-lin?eref=FromFacebookShare (accessed March 1, 2012).

8. Ibid.

9. "Jeremy Lin: The New Steve Nash, Making Asian-American History Tonight in Santa Clara, of All Places," goldenstateofmind.com, January 4, 2010, www.goldenstateofmind.com/2010/1/4/1232730/ jeremy-lin-the-new-steve-nash (accessed March 1, 2012).

10. Pablo S. Torre, "Harvard School of Basketball," *Sports Illustrated*, February 1, 2010, http://si.com/vault/article/magazine/MAG1165302/ index.htm (accessed March 1, 2012).

11. Ed Welland, "NBA Draft Preview 2010: Jeremy Lin, G Harvard," hoopsanalyst.com, May 13, 2010, http://goo.gl/fGJwv (accessed March 1, 2012).

12. Tim Kawakami, "Lacob Interview: Part 3," *San Jose Mercury News*, August 17, 2010, http://blogs.mercurynews.com/kawakami/2010/08/17/ lacob-interview-part–3-on-jeremy-lin-ellison-larry-riley-bold-moves- and-poker/ (accessed March 1, 2012).

13. Samantha Gilman, "Sustaining Faith," *World*, February 16, 2012, www.worldmag.com/webextra/19193 (accessed March 1, 2012).

14. Quoted in Gilman, "Sustaining Faith."

15. Ibid.

16. Dan Duggan, "Jeremy Lin's Teammates Are Enjoying 'Linsanity' as Much as Anyone," *Boston Herald*, February 17, 2012, www.boston herald.com/blogs/sports/oncampus/?p=415 (accessed March 1, 2012).

17. Tim Keown, "Jeremy Lin's HS Coach Is Surprised, Too," espn.com, February 14, 2012, http://espn.go.com/espn/commentary/story/_/ id/7574452/jeremy-lin-high-school-coach-surprised-too (accessed March 1, 2012).

18. Daniel Brown, "Bay Area Trainers Helped Make Knicks Guard Jeremy Lin Better, Stronger, Faster," *San Jose Mercury News*, February 23, 2012, www.mercurynews.com/top-stories/ci_20033514 (accessed March 1, 2012).

19. Marcus Thompson II, "Jeremy Lin's Story Has Been a Story of Faith," *Contra Costa Times*, February 13, 2012, www.ibabuzz.com/ warriors/2012/02/13/jeremy-lins-journey-has-been-a-story-of-faith/ (accessed March 1, 2012).

20. Michael Moraitis, "New York Knicks: Jeremy Lin Isn't the Only Right Move GM Glen Grunwald Has Made," bleacherreport.com, February 22, 2012, http://goo.gl/zlFtU (accessed March 1, 2012).

21. Sean Brennan, "Knicks Claim Harvard Grad Off Waivers," *New York Daily News*, December 27, 2011, http://goo.gl/lGhQm (accessed March 1, 2012).

22. Erik Qualman, "Jeremy Lin: Lin-Sanity Hits Twitter @JLin7," social

NOTES

nomics.com, February 15, 2012, www.socialnomics.net/2012/02/15/ jeremy-lin-lin-sanity-hits-twitter-jlin7/ (accessed March 1, 2012).

23. The painting by Greg Olsen is titled *Lost and Found*. In Olsen's description, he wrote, "Many of us have probably asked ... 'What about me?' What about those of us who may have struggled and lost our way, or who have wandered paths that have left us worn and doubting our worth? Thankfully, Christ's love carries no conditions and is extended in full measure, especially to those who feel lost and forgotten."

24. Jeff Zillgitt, "Jeremy Lin, Humbled, Humorous during All-Star Weekend," *USA Today*, February 25, 2012, www.usatoday.com/sports/ basketball/nba/knicks/story/2012-02-25/jermey-lin-all-star-weekend/ 53244342/1 (accessed March 1, 2012).

25. Quoted in Thompson, "Jeremy Lin's Story Has Been a Story of Faith."

26. Frank Isola, "Lin, Knicks Scale Wall's Wizards in Washington," *New York Daily News*, February 8, 2012, http://goo.gl/FGH8o (accessed March 1, 2012).

27. Howard Beck, "Lin Leads Again as Knicks Win 3rd in a Row," *New York Times*, February 8, 2012, http://goo.gl/9eD9I (accessed March 1, 2012).

28. Tim Stelloh and Noah Rosenberg, "From the Pulpit and in the Pew, the Knicks' Lin Is a Welcome Inspiration," *New York Times*, February 12, 2012, http://goo.gl/DHLnw (accessed March 1, 2012).

29. Kevin Armstrong, "Jeremy Lin: The True Hollywood Story of the Knick Sensation Who's Taken Over New York in Less Than a Week," *New York Daily News*, February 11, 2012, http://articles.nydailynews .com/2012-02-11/news/31051048_1_jeremy-lin-knicks-landry-fields (accessed March 1, 2012).

30. Austin Knoblauch, "*Saturday Night Live* Weighs In on Jeremy Lin Story" (skit, broadcast on February 18, 2012), www.latimes.com/ sports/sportsnow/la-sp-sn-snl-jeremy-lin-20120220,0,3318283.story (accessed March 1, 2012).

31. "Jeremy Lin's Religious Pregame Ritual," thestar.com (February 13, 2012), http://goo.gl/CeKvW (accessed March 1, 2012).

32. David Jackson, "Obama: Heard of Lin 'Way Back When,'" *USA Today*, March 1, 2012, http://goo.gl/AQOQC (accessed March 1, 2012).

33. William Wong, "Linsanity 3: Will Fame Ruin Jeremy Lin?" sfgate.com, February 17, 2012, http://goo.gl/XPhiH (accessed March 1, 2012).

34. **James Brown:** Armen Keteyian, "Jeremy Lin: New York Knicks' Cinderella Story," CBS.com, February 15, 2012, http://goo.gl/hFFL5 (accessed March 1, 2012).

David Brooks: David Brooks, "The Jeremy Lin Problem," *New York Times*, February 16, 2012, http://goo.gl/S0XYZ (accessed March 1, 2012).

Christine Folch: Tim Stelloh and Noah Rosenberg, "From the Pulpit and in the Pew, the Knicks' Lin Is a Welcome Inspiration," *New York Times*, February 12, 2012, http://goo.gl/DHLnw (accessed March 1, 2012).

Earvin "Magic" Johnson: statement during halftime show of the Knicks-Mavericks game on ABC, February 19, 2012.

Bill Plaschke: *Los Angeles Times* sports section, February 21, 2012, page C1.

Bryan Harvey: Margo Adler, "Knicks Star Jeremy Lin Captures Big Apple's Heart," npr.com, February 16, 2012, www.npr.org/2012/02/16/146958259/knicks-star-jeremy-lin-captures-big-apples-heart (accessed March 1, 2012).

Stephen Curry: Rusty Simmons, "Mark Jackson Recalls Departure of Jeremy Lin," sfgate.com, February 13, 2012, www.sfgate.com/cgi-bin/article.cgi?f=/c/a/2012/02/12/SPH01N6MPK.DTL (accessed March 1, 2012).

35. Jeff Zillgitt, "Jeremy Lin Scores 26, but Hornets Snap Knicks' Win Streak," *USA Today*, February 16, 2012, http://goo.gl/GWvum (accessed March 1, 2012).

36. Amy Shipley, "Jeremy Lin Fails to Lift Knicks Over LeBron's Miami Heat," *Washington Post*, February 24, 2012, http://goo.gl/9tJai (accessed March 1, 2012).

37. Richard Hoffer, "Over in a New York Minute," *Sports Illustrated*, March 26, 2012, http://sportsillustrated.cnn.com/vault/article/magazine/MAG1196292/index.htm (accessed November 26, 2012).

38. Will Leitch, "Rocket Man," *GQ*, November 2012, www.gq.com/sports/profiles/201211/jeremy-lin-gq-november-2012-cover-story (accessed November 26, 2012).

39. Matt Moore, "Knicks Acquire Felton in Sign-and-Trade with Blazers," CBS Sports.com, July 14, 2012, www.cbssports.com/nba/blog/eye-on-basketball/19587022 (accessed November 26, 2012).

40. "New York Post Lays Off Its 32-Person Jeremy Lin Pun Staff," sportspickle.com, July 16, 2012, www.sportspickle.com/news/13195/new-york-post-lays-off-its-32-person-jeremy-lin-pun-staff (accessed November 26, 2012).

41. Marcus Thompson II, "Jeremy Lin Exclusive: I Will Always Have Haters," *San Jose Mercury News*, July 23, 2012.

42. Quoted in Christine Thomasos, "James Harden Wanted Time to

Pray before Leaving OKC," *Christian Post*, November 7, 2012, www
.christianpost.com/news/james-harden-wanted-time-to-pray-before-
leaving-okc-84599/ (accessed November 26, 2012).

43. Irv Soonachan, "Point of Attention: Rookie Jeremy Lin Has Proven
He Can Play in the NBA," slamonline.com, April 5, 2011, www.
slamonline.com/online/nba/2011/04/point-of-attention/ (accessed
March 1, 2012).

44. See "Jeremy Lin's Late-Night Escape in Taipei," 60 Minutes Overtime,
September 6, 2012, www.cbsnews.com/8301-504803_162-57507801-
10391709/jeremy-lins-late-night-escape-in-taipei/ (accessed November
26, 2012).

45. Madison Park, "Asian Fans Cheer 'Linsanity," CNN, August 24, 2012,
www.cnn.com/2012/08/24/world/jeremy-lin-hong-kong/index.html
(accessed November 26, 2012).

46. Sally Jenkins, "Bill Maher and Tim Tebow: Why Are So Many
Offended by the Quarterback's Faith?" *Washington Post*, December 30,
2011, http://goo.gl/5ioHE (accessed March 1, 2012).

47. "Jeremy Lin: Taking Harvard Basketball to New Levels," StudentSoul
.org, March 12, 2010, www.intervarsity.org/studentsoul/item/jeremy-
lin?eref=FromFacebookShare (accessed March 1, 2012).

48. "Tim Tebow: God Doesn't Love Athletes More," CBS News, January 13,
2012, http://goo.gl/LL8ET (accessed March 1, 2012).

49. Dan Duggan, "Always Believe–Lin," *Boston Herald*, February 17, 2012,
http://goo.gl/rBqb4 (accessed March 1, 2012).

50. Jill Baughman, "Jeremy Lin + Tim Tebow = Cutest Sports Bromance
Ever," Cafemom.com, February 23, 2012, http://thestir.cafemom.com/
sports/133481/jeremy_lin_tim_tebow_cutest (accessed March 1, 2012).

51. Kevin Armstrong, "Jeremy Lin: The True Hollywood Story of the
Knick Sensation Who's Taken Over New York in Less Than a Week,"
New York Daily News, February 11, 2012, http://articles.nydailynews
.com/2012–02–11/news/31051048_1_jeremy-lin-knicks-landry-fields
(accessed March 1, 2012).

52. Mike Vaccaro, "Lin Had Prayer Answered after First Knicks-Heat
Matchup," *New York Post*, February 23, 2012, http://goo.gl/63kzt
(accessed March 1, 2012).

53. Jared Zwerling, "NBA Holds Press Conference Just for Lin," espn.com,
February 24, 2012, http://goo.gl/TNNXY (accessed March 1, 2012).

Share Your Thoughts

With the Author: Your comments will be forwarded to the author when you send them to *zauthor@zondervan.com*.

With Zondervan: Submit your review of this book by writing to *zreview@zondervan.com*.

Free Online Resources at
www.zondervan.com

Zondervan AuthorTracker: Be notified whenever your favorite authors publish new books, go on tour, or post an update about what's happening in their lives at www.zondervan.com/authortracker.

Daily Bible Verses and Devotions: Enrich your life with daily Bible verses or devotions that help you start every morning focused on God. Visit www.zondervan.com/newsletters.

Free Email Publications: Sign up for newsletters on Christian living, academic resources, church ministry, fiction, children's resources, and more. Visit www.zondervan.com/newsletters.

Zondervan Bible Search: Find and compare Bible passages in a variety of translations at www.zondervanbiblesearch.com.

Other Benefits: Register to receive online benefits like coupons and special offers, or to participate in research.

ZONDERVAN.com/
AUTHORTRACKER
follow your favorite authors